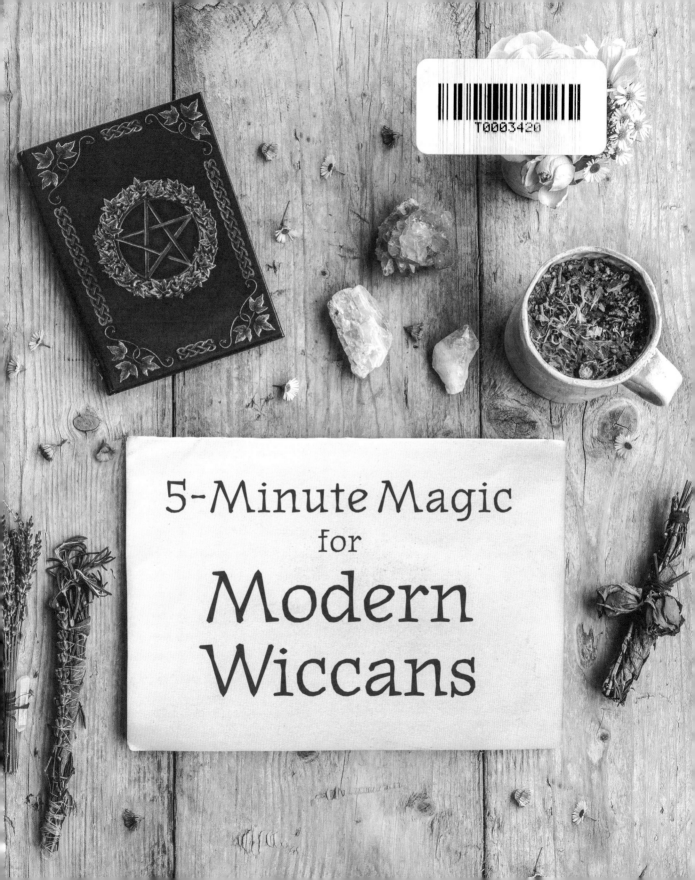

5-Minute Magic
for
Modern
Wiccans

5-Minute Magic for
Modern Wiccans

Rapid rituals, efficient enchantments,
and swift spells

CERRIDWEN GREENLEAF

CICO BOOKS

LONDON NEW YORK

"Pick up your rattle, pack up your dreams.
We'll walk hand-in-hand in a magical land."
Luisah Teish

**This book is for all the grandmothers, wise women, elders, crones
and other women who have passed down the wisdom we use today.
Eternal love and gratitude.**

This edition published in 2022 by CICO Books
An imprint of Ryland Peters & Small Ltd

20–21 Jockey's Fields   341 E 116th St
London WC1R 4BW   New York, NY 10029
www.rylandpeters.com

10 9 8 7 6 5 4 3 2 1

First published in 2019

A CIP catalog record for this book is available from the
Library of Congress and the British Library.

ISBN: 978-1-80065-158-6

Printed in China

Editor: Sophie Elletson
Photographer and stylist: Belle Daughtry

Commissioning editor: Kristine Pidkameny
Senior editor: Carmel Edmonds
Designer: Eliana Holder and Emily Breen
Art director: Sally Powell
Production controller: Mai-Ling Collyer
Publishing manager: Penny Craig
Publisher: Cindy Richards

Safety note: Please note that while the use of
essential oils, herbs, incense, and particular practices
refer to healing benefits, they are not intended to
replace diagnosis of illness or ailments, or healing or
medicine. Always consult your doctor or other health
professional in the case of illness, pregnancy, and
personal sensitivities and conditions. Neither the
author not the publisher can be held responsible for
any claim arising out of the general information,
recipes, and practices provided in the book.

FSC
www.fsc.org

MIX
Paper from
responsible sources
FSC® C106563

Contents

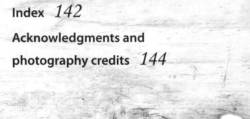

Introduction:
More Magic in Less Time

Let's face it: we are all overscheduled. Even children and teens need planners and calendar reminders to keep up with all the activities that are part of a modern busy life. Meanwhile, our devices are beeping, buzzing, and constantly reminding us of all we have to do. What's a busy witch to do? I contend that magic is the ultimate self-help and is also wonderfully creative self-care. While there may not be quite as much time nowadays for daily spells and rites that last many hours—you can save those for high holidays, Full Moon festivals, and other group gatherings—you can lead just as magical a life with incantations and enchantments that match the pace of a twenty-first-century pagan lifestyle. Just 5 minutes of everyday magic can bring much meaning into your life, along with the enormous benefits of brighter health, greater prosperity, lasting love, good luck, and that sense of wholeness that can only come from a balance between your mind, body, and spirit.

This book is very much a response to what I've been hearing from you, dear readers, in all your letters, emails, Facebook messages, and blog comments. Message received, loud and clear! You want more magic in less time for your very busy and very blessed lives. Thanks to your excellent input, this set of spells is steeped in ancient wisdom yet updated for the modern day; it has an emphasis on maximum manifestation in the minimum amount of time. In this book, for the first time, I take time-tested magical workings with a quick turnaround that offer real results. All the rituals here are based on the practice of Wicca, the twentieth-century wisdom tradition based on witchcraft of yore. Here, we are adding a further modern touch, updating for these busy times.

This is an all-purpose spellbook with many magical rituals and charms that you can apply to every aspect of your life: health, wealth, work, creativity, home and family, self-care and love. This also builds upon my earliest spellwork, which was simple, direct, and designed for a fast result. When I was younger, I wanted everything in a hurry! Nowadays, people are busier than ever and are asking for expeditious rites and spells. I agree with you, my fellow Wiccans, that now is the time for a quickening of magic!

The Witch's Toolkit: *Everything You Need to Know for Making Fast Magic*

Welcome to the world of fast magic! One of the best ways to set the stage for rapid rituals and efficient enchantments is to plan ahead and shop smart, which is easy to do, even with our busy modern lifestyles. Nowadays, there are amazing candles and essential oils at the grocer, pharmacy, and apothecary store; cord at the craft store; incense, herbs, and crystals aplenty at the mind-body bookshop and health-food store; and metaphysical must-haves are around every corner. I, for one, can hardly believe that witchy cinnamon brooms can be found at Trader Joe's and Bed Bath and Beyond, and online. All of this makes it simple to speed up your spellcraft and sail down the express lane to a happier life infused with magic every step of the way. The spells and ritual work in this book cover the gamut and there's truly something for everyone, from beginners to those of you who are very advanced in your wielding of the craft. This section is intended to cover the basics and provide tools and knowledge to prepare the way for making fast magic.

Your Essential Tools

Your *altar* is the center of your enchantments, your personal power space. A Wiccan altar is where you place symbolic and functional items for the purpose of spells and ritual work as well as a space for speaking chants and prayers. Your altar can— and should—evolve and change with the seasons.

Your *Book of Shadows* is a journal of your choosing in which you write down your magical workings and notes. When you track the effectiveness of a ritual, you can use this to refine your spellcraft in the future and your power will increase.

Candles are truly essential and contain all four of the elemental energies:

* *Air*—Oxygen feeds and fans the candle flame.
* *Earth*—The solid wax forms the candle.
* *Water*—Melted wax is the fluid elemental state.
* *Fire*—The flame sparks and blazes.

You can "dress" or anoint the candle with a couple of drops of essential oil on the side of the candle using a dropper or cotton ball. Go with your instinct on choosing sizes, shapes, and colors. I recommend keeping an array of options on hand. Different candle colors can enhance your spells and many of the rituals in this book suggest specific colors.

Magical knives: An athame (pronounced "a-*thaw*-may") is your magical knife and should be placed on the right side of your altar. The athame is used to direct the energies raised in your ritual and usually has a dull blade. Since black is the color that absorbs energy, athames should have a dark handle. A bolline is a white-handled knife that is used for making other tools and for cutting materials, such as cords and herbs, within a magic circle. You can cut a branch to create your wand, for example.

Brooms (or "besoms") have certainly captured the popular imagination as the emblem of witches. Using a broom as a magical tool came about from sweeping the ritual area clean before and after casting a spell. Now they're mostly used in symbolic energy management.

Cauldrons represent the Goddess (also called Source or divine power), their round basins symbolizing the womb from whence all comes. A cast iron cauldron can hold fire and can even be used to burn incense or purifying sage. You can place a cauldron on your altar if there is room, or on the floor to the left of the altar.

Essential oils are natural oils made by distillations of herbs and flowers, ideally organic. They retain the fragrance of the original plant from which they are made. When you are making a blend of oils or a potion or lotion, mix them with a carrier (or base) oil, such as jojoba, almond, apricot, grapeseed, or sesame, to dilute the essential oil and make it safe to apply to the skin. Always test a blend on a small area of the skin first and leave for 24 hours to check you don't have any reaction to it.

Magical Meanings of Essential Oils

* *Psychic power:* jasmine, benzoin, cinnamon, sandalwood

* *Courage:* geranium, black pepper, frankincense

* *Dispelling negative energy and spirits:* basil, clove, copal, frankincense, juniper, myrrh, pine, peppermint, rosemary, Solomon's seal, yarrow, vervain

* *Divination:* camphor, orange, clove

* *Enchantment:* ginger, tangerine, amber, apple

* *Healing:* bay, cedar wood, cinnamon, coriander, eucalyptus, juniper, lime, rose, sandalwood, spearmint

* *Joy:* lavender, neroli, bergamot, vanilla

* *Love:* apricot, basil, chamomile, clove, copal, coriander, rose, geranium, jasmine, lemon, lime, neroli, rosemary, ylang-ylang

* *Luck:* orange, nutmeg, rose, vervain

* *Peace:* lavender, chamomile

* *Prosperity:* basil, clove, ginger, cinnamon, nutmeg, orange, oak, moss, patchouli, peppermint, pine, aloe

* *Protection:* bay, anise, black pepper, cedar, clove, cypress, copal, eucalyptus, frankincense, rose geranium, lime, myrrh, lavender, juniper, sandalwood, vetiver

* *Sexuality:* cardamom, lemongrass, amber, rose, clove, olive, patchouli

Incense contains inherent energies that you can use to further your intention and promote your purpose. Every New Age store, herb shop, or health food store has a wide variety of cone, stick, and loose incense. Many spells call for creating your own incense mixture, best done by grinding the incense ingredients in a mortar and pestle. You can then store the fine powder in small sealable jars. Craft stores and New Age shops carry the 4-ounce (115ml) lidded jars that are perfect for DIY incenses. This kind of powdered or loose incense needs to be burned on a charcoal cake, usually sold in these same stores in packets of ten. You should set the charcoals in a fireproof glass or clay dish or use your censer from which the smoke will waft out enchantingly. Another kind of sacred smoke you will come to rely on is when you burn sage to purify and clear a space. Sage bundles are readily available at any New Age shop and are essential to keep on hand for much of your ritual work.

A *censer*, also called a thurible, is an incense burner and represents the elements of Air and Fire. Place your censer at the center of your altar. Incense can be used to purify your other sacred tools and to cleanse your ritual space.

A *pendulum* is a witchy tool that helps with decision making. Pendulums are easily bought at any metaphysical or New Age shop or mind, body, spirit bookstore, but you can also make your own, with a 12-inch (30cm) strip of string or leather cord and a small rose quartz with a pointy end. Knot the quartz onto your cord and test it to show you which is "yes" and which is "no." This is done by asking it yes/no questions that you know the answer to, then observing its responses— you will notice it swings in a different way for each one, for example, round in a circle clockwise or anticlockwise, or back and forth.

Keep *cord and string* in different colors for use in your spellwork—a magic cord is a rope that binds you to magic. I like silken cords as they feel good in your hands and are lovely, but knitting yarn makes for nice string and comes in an endless array of magical hues.

Potpourri is a hedge witch and herbalist's staple for floral spellcraft. Similarly, you should have a collection of dried flowers, petals, and herbs and mix them into combinations with special energies.

Wands are conduits of energy and your personal magic; as such, yours should be a very special tool either made or chosen with care. Find out more overleaf.

Make Your Own Manifestation Tool

A wand is used for directing energy. It is best to make your own wand from found wood and instill it with your personal energy. You could go out into a nearby park or the woods and find a suitable branch that has fallen. Never cut a wand straight from a tree as the energy from harm to the tree will be retained by the wand. Allow Mother Nature to choose one for you; she is always right. You might find the perfect weathered wand on a beach as driftwood.

Gather together

* ☆ a found piece of wood (see suggestions below)
* ☆ sand paper
* ☆ bolline
* ☆ 12 inches (30cm) copper wire
* ☆ a crystal of your preference to use as the pointer (see page 114 for suggestions)
* ☆ beads, sequins, seashells, tiny crystals, or other decorations of your choice

When you have found the perfect piece of wood, sand it to smoothness so it feels good in your hand, which is very important. If your found wood branch is too long, use your magical bolline knife to cut it down to 12 inches (30cm), or your preferred length. Wrap copper wire around the top and affix your crystal to the end. Your wand should look beautiful to your eye so embellish it with ornaments you love, such as beads, sequins, seashells, tiny crystals, or whatever pleases you and adds to the power of this sacred implement.

When choosing wood for your wand, remember that each tree has distinctive properties:

* *Birch* (*Betula pendula*) has feminine energy and healing power. Boiled soft birch wood was traditionally used to soothe bruises and calm cuts. Use a birch wand for healing spells, for calming situations, and for requesting a diplomatic solution.

* *Crab apple* (*Malus sylvestris*) will provide bent, gnarled wands. The apple tree, as we know, is the tree of knowledge and wisdom. Apples, the fruit and the wood, are extremely useful to witchcraft. Use an apple wand whenever you need guidance, want to know the truth, or simply as an everyday wand.

* *Rowan* or *mountain ash* (*Sorbus aucuparia*) is native to the British Isles. There is a closely related American species, *Sorbus Americana*. It's a "portal tree," and therefore when you want to undertake a journey or a guided visualization, keep your mountain-ash wand close by.

* *Oak* (*Quercus robur*) has a strong masculine energy and is good for healing and protection. It makes a long-lasting wand for intensely focused work. If you choose to use only one wand, make it oak.

There are other suggestions for materials to make wands in this book—see pages 53, 80, and 97.

Bringing Magic into Your Life

When you establish a sacred space, such as your altar, and use your magical tools in it, you can create a place where the mundane world is left behind. It can be in your home or your backyard where, despite the noise of the day-to-day, you can touch the sacred. Anywhere you choose can become a circle of magic and you can create one anywhere by "casting," or drawing in the air with concentrated energy with a wand or athame. Inside this circle, energy is raised, rituals are performed, and spells are worked. The sacred space is also where you call upon the gods and goddesses and become attuned to your own special desires. With attention and focus, working in the circle can be a truly marvelous experience. All your senses will come alive. You will feel, see, and hear the energies that you invoke. You will have created a tangible sphere of power.

Trust your intuition, go with your instincts, and listen to your heart.

By following these three simple guidelines, you will craft beautiful, and more importantly, meaningful rituals to enrich your life, provide comfort, and maintain harmony and balance in your life. Personal ritual benefits you the most when it adapts to your current needs. Whether you need serenity, prosperity, more love in your life or swift change, the spells in this book will help you get there. And faster!

Chapter 1

Everyday Lunar and Solar Spells:
Use Moon and Sun Power for Magic

Most of us learn early on that certain phases of the moon and solar months have special significance simply by hearing about astrology and your personal sun sign. Whether you believe in astrology or not, you probably know your sign, and even a bit about what that is supposed to mean. There certainly is deep meaning behind it and we will explore that significance here and what it offers you.

It is not just us spiritual folk who believe in all this, either. Millions of farmers and dedicated gardeners have used astrological knowledge gleaned from sources like *The Old Farmer's Almanac*, as well as their own records, which, time and again, back up ancient wisdom. This wisdom remains of vital importance in our modern times. Applying it to your own life will bring you many rewards over time, too.

Here, you can learn which sun signs, moon signs, and lunar phases are best for your magical workings, optimal for outings, perfect for romance, ideal for job prospects, most favorable for creative pursuits, and hold the highest probability for success in any venture, whether it be a social gathering, ritual, or painstaking project. Of equal importance is knowing when *not* to do something. I have learned the hard way from planting costly fruit trees at the wrong time and watched as they withered and died for seemingly no reason. These same principles apply to most areas of life. Timing is everything and most certainly for spells, rites, rituals, and charms.

Your Moon Phase Guide

The proper phase of the moon is essential for spellcraft. Each lunar cycle begins with a "new" phase when the moon lies between the sun and the earth so the illuminated side cannot be seen from earth. The moon gradually "waxes" until it has moved to the opposite side of the earth, and its lit side faces us in the "full" moon phase. It then begins to "wane" until it reaches the new moon phase again. The entire cycle takes around a month, during which the moon orbits the earth.

Performing a spell at the optimal time in the lunar cycle will maximize your power. As you read the spells in this book, keep this essential approach to magic in mind.

How to match your spells to moon phases

★ The *new moon* is an auspicious time for a fresh start.

★ The *crescent moon*, which appears seven days before and after the new moon, is the time for productivity and creating positive energy.

★ While *waxing*, the moon grows steadily larger and is good for spellwork toward completing goals and building toward an outcome.

★ The *full moon* is a great teacher with a special message for each month.

★ The *waning moon* is the time to wind down any personal challenges and see them to an end.

New Moon, New Friends

When I moved to San Francisco, I didn't know a soul, but I used this tried-and-tested trick to fill my life with friends.

Gather together

* ☆ 1 candle of any color or size
* ☆ your favorite incense

Timing: Try this on a new moon Friday (Freya's Day, which is ruled by Venus, is ideal for fun, love, flirtation, gossip, and good times).

Light the candle and incense. Breath in the sacred smoke and dance around, arms held upward, joyously. Say aloud:

I call upon you, friend Freya,
To fill my life with love and joy. I call upon you, Goddess,
To bring unto me that which I enjoy
In the form of people, wise and kind.
This I ask and give thanks for, blessed be.

This resulted in me having friends who have stuck with me through thick and thin; I can count on them for boundless love and they bring so much joy to my life.

Inspired Clarity: *Breath of the Gods Incense*

Burn this mixture of incense on your altar to generate a positive and peaceful atmosphere to set the stage for your ritual. Rose hips and mint are for heart, enthusiasm, and keen thinking. The yellow candle, yellow rose, and the yellow citrine crystal are used to symbolize intelligence and mental clarity.

Gather together

* ☆ 1 tablespoon dried rose hips
* ☆ 1 teaspoon fresh or dried mint
* ☆ a charcoal cake for burning incense
* ☆ a fireproof clay or glass dish
* ☆ a yellow candle
* ☆ neroli essential oil
* ☆ a yellow rose bud
* ☆ 1 cup (240ml) of fresh water in a bowl
* ☆ a citrine crystal

Timing: Perform this rite during the new moon, when the moon is dark and not visible.

Using your mortar and pestle, grind together the rose hips and the mint. Once they are nicely mixed, place the herbs on a piece of charcoal in a fireproof clay or glass dish. Light a yellow candle anointed with neroli oil and place a single yellow rose in a vase to one side of the incense burner. On the other side, place the bowl of water with the citrine crystal in it. Light the incense and breathe in. The word "inspire" comes from the Greek word for "breath of the gods," so allow this divine essence to fill you with grace.

Crescent Moon Magic

This is the perfect time to lay plans for all good things you desire in this phase of increasing.

Gather together

★ a pure white garment

★ a moonstone of any size

★ a short piece of string

Timing: The ideal phase for this spell is when the crescent moon is waxing.

In the first quarter of the moon, don your white shirt or dress, and carry the moonstone along with you in your pocket or on a pendant. Take a late afternoon walk in a park or a meadow among wild weeds, flowers and grasses, and gather a few as you stroll to make a bouquet. Choose a resting place and sit where you can see the crescent moon. Take your flowers and grasses and bind them with the string. Hold your newly made bouquet in your right hand. Hold your moonstone in your left hand and concentrate on your desired outcome—creative fulfillment, greater happiness, or perhaps the release of anger. Chant aloud:

Luna, in your seventh heaven, I invoke you now.
Brighter than any star, you are.
I will sing your magic song, if you but show me how.
I will walk your sacred path, if you but show me where.
Be here now.

Arms outspread, eyes on the moon, repeat the chant three times. As the moon shines brighter, so will your spirit.

Recharging Weekend Wonder: *Natural Remedy Potion*

This natural remedy is an excellent way to refresh after a hectic week.

Gather together

★ 2 drops rosemary essential oil

★ 3 drops bergamot essential oil

★ 2 drops jasmine essential oil

★ 3 drops lavender essential oil

★ 6 drops carrier oil

★ a small ceramic or glass bowl

Timing: This tincture is most potent right after the sun sets, by the light of the waxing or full moon.

Blend the essential oils and carrier oil in the bowl. Take off your shoes so you can be more grounded. Walk outside, stand on your deck or by an open window. Now, close your eyes, lift your head to the moon, and recite aloud:

Bright moon goddess, eternal and wise,
Give your strength to me now.
As I breathe, you are alive in me for this night.
Health to all, calm to me.
So mote it be.

Gently rub one drop of Natural Remedy Potion on each pulse point: both wrists, behind your ear lobes, on the base of your neck, and behind your knees. As the oil surrounds you with its warm scent, you will be filled with a quiet strength.

Lunar Elixir: *Restorative Full Moon Infusion*

The full moon is a truly auspicious time and one to savor and make the most of. Try this restorative Lunar Elixir anytime your energy level is low to bolster mind, body, and spirit.

Gather together

★ 1 teaspoon sliced fresh ginger root

★ 1 teaspoon jasmine tea leaves

★ 1 teaspoon peppermint tea leaves

★ 2 cups (480ml) fresh water

★ a teapot and a mug

Timing: Full moon phases last two days, so make this elixir on the first night at midnight.

Just before midnight, brew and strain an infusion of these healthful and energizing herbs. Once it is cool, pour it into your favorite mug and relish the aromatic steam for a moment. Wait for the stroke of midnight. Now, step outside and drink the elixir during this enchanted hour in the glow of moonlight. You will immediately feel clearer, more centered, and more focused.

Don't Worry, Be Happy: *A Spell to Quell Anxiety*

As the sun sets on a waning moon day, you can quiet the inner voices of worrywart that get in the way of life. When our moon ebbs, another grows forth, and so it goes for our creativity and renewal cycles.

Gather together

* ★ 1 vanilla bean pod
* ★ sandalwood incense
* ★ amber resin
* ★ a charcoal cake for burning incense
* ★ a fireproof glass or clay dish
* ★ 1 black or gray candle

Timing: As the moon decreases in size, cast this spell.

Quick Tip:
Moon Spell Secrets

In late spring and early summer, you will see a shape resembling a dragon on the moon—an auspicious time for new beginnings, business, and magic related to work and money. The moon dragon is visible when Jupiter occupies the center of the sky. Ventures begun under its influence will meet with great success.

Set aside a small piece of the vanilla bean, then grind together a teaspoon each of sandalwood, amber, and the remainder of the vanilla bean using either the back of a spoon or your mortar and pestle. Burn this resin-based mixture on a piece of charcoal in the fireproof dish on your altar. Light the black or gray candle, for protection. Rub the reserved small piece of vanilla bean in your palm until the scent begins to waft up thanks to the heat in your hands. Concentrate on the flame and rub the same vanilla essence on your temples and place your hand over your heart.

As you meditate, think about how you sometimes doubt yourself, worry needlessly, and how you will begin to trust your innate wisdom and instincts. Visualize clearing all anxiety from your mind. Think about the wonderful aspects in your life, your bright future, and your potential as you chant:

La lune, goddess of the moon,
As you may grow, so do I.
Here, tonight, under your darkest light,
I embrace all within me that is good and right,
and bid goodbye to all the rest. Blessed be.

Blow out the candle and throw it into a fireplace or your cast iron cauldron to burn away. You must completely destroy the candle because it contains the energy of your anxiety and fear. Now, go and worry no more.

Waning Moon Contentment Ritual

You can create a week of blissful and composed calm with
the following spell.

Gather together

* ☆ a purple candle
* ☆ hibiscus or violet essential oil
* ☆ a bouquet of purple flowers
  (violets, for example)

Timing: On a Monday, as the moon
grows smaller in the sky, try this spell.

On a waning moon Monday evening, anoint your purple candle
with the essential oil. Place the candle on your altar beside a vase
of fresh violets or other purple flowers. Sit in front of your altar as
twilight begins, and when the sun is completely gone, light the
candle and chant:

Any care and despair begone.
Here with the mountain, the river, the tree, the grass
and the moon.
I receive my strength from Nature and she is my center.
Tomorrow and the next, all gladness will enter.
Harm to none, only good.

Lunar and Solar Sign Connections

When the sun or moon is in a certain zodiac sign, it carries that astrological energy. The zodiacal year starts with the sun in Aries, usually on March 21, and the sun then goes through all twelve astrological signs each month. The moon moves more quickly than the sun and stays in a sign for two days before moving on to the next.

You might notice you feel highly energetic one day and more laid back the next. Why is that? Look to the moon for answers. I recommend consulting a reliable source for tracking the sign of the moon—see Resources, page 141. Keep track in your Book of Shadows of the effect that these solar and lunar connections have for you. You can further enhance these astrological associations by using the associated crystals and colors for your candles with the energy of these signs—see the chart below.

Aries, Mars-ruled sign of the Ram, is a high-energy time, which is good for new beginnings. Associated with diamond, amethyst, topaz, garnet, iron, and steel, and the color red.

Venus-ruled *Taurus* is the Bull and is very abundant in all ways: money, farming, and love. Associated with coral, sapphire, emerald, turquoise, agate, zircon, and copper, and the color azure.

Gemini is ruled by Mercury and is about smarts, quickness, communication, and travel. Associated with aquamarine, agate, amber, emerald, topaz, and aluminum, and the color electric blue.

Lunar *Cancer* is connected with family and home, and is most fertile of all for farming. Associated with opal, pearl, emerald, moonstone, and silver, and the colors pearl and rose.

Leo is ruled by the sun and it is romantic, brave, showy, and a time to lead. Associated with diamond, ruby, gold, sardonyx, and chrysoberyl, and the color orange.

Mercury-ruled *Virgo* is good for health, nutrition, and detailed hard work. Associated with jade, rhodonite, sapphire, carnelian, and aluminum, and the color gray-blue.

Libra is ruled by Venus and is artistic, loving, abundant, and balancing. Associated with opal, sapphire, jade, quartz, turquoise, and copper, and the color pale orange.

Plutonic *Scorpio* is very sensual and sexual, bountiful, and a time for strategy. Associated with bloodstone, topaz, aquamarine, jasper, and silver, and the color dark red.

Jupiter-ruled *Sagittarius* connotes philosophy, spirituality, treks, and higher understanding. Associated with lapis lazuli, topaz, turquoise, coral, and tin, and the color purple.

Earth-ruled *Capricorn* is good for business, money, jobs, goals, and politics. Associated with onyx, jet, ruby, lead, and malachite, and the color brown.

Uranus-ruled *Aquarius* is a time for intellect, risk, innovation, and interaction. Associated with aquamarine, jade, fluorite, sapphire, zircon, and aluminum, and the color green.

Neptune-ruled *Pisces* is for psychism, dreams, affection, and creativity. Associated with amethyst, alexandrite, bloodstone, stitchite, and silver, and the color ocean blue.

For Insights and Ideas: *Element of Air Tonic*

This spell should give you brilliant insight, enabling you to
see with great peace and clarity.

Gather together

☆ 1 tablespoon fenugreek seeds

☆ 4 tablespoons fresh peppermint
leaves

☆ a pinch of dried lavender

☆ a yellow teapot

☆ honey

Timing: Perform this spell when
the new moon is in an Air sign:
Aquarius, Gemini, or Libra.

Steep the herbs in boiling water in your sunny yellow teapot;
yellow is one of the colors associated with mental prowess. After
5 minutes, sweeten with honey, and either drink the mild tea while
facing east, the source of the rising sun, or mark the four directions
and pour the tea on the ground outside toward the east, praying:

Winged Mercury, God of air,
I entreat you to bring me sight and true awareness.
Like the wind, speed my way.

Make everything new.

Listen to your intuition now; it will not fail you.

Gratitude Prayer Spell

Gratitude is not only uplifting but feels wonderful. There is powerful magic in recognizing all that you possess.

Timing: When moon or sun is in the sign of Taurus it is the time of prosperity and security. Time this ritual for a Thursday during that lunar or solar sign as Thursday is "Thor's Day" and the day of abundance. It is also the perfect time to acknowledge the gifts of life.

Sit in a comfortable position and close your eyes. Think about your blessings. What are you grateful for at this moment? Breathe steadily and deeply, inhaling and exhaling slowly for a few minutes. Now pray aloud:

Good gods and Goddess, giver of all the fruits of this earth,
Thank you for all bounty, beauty, and well-being,
Bless all who give and receive these gifts.
I am made of sacred earth, purest water, sacred fire, and wildest wind.
Blessings upon me. Blessings upon we and thee.
So mote it be.

Record your blessings in a journal or in your Book of Shadows. You should perform this gratitude prayer spell periodically and look back at your blessings and reflect upon them. This is also a wonderful grace to say at the family meal to offer thanks for all we are given.

Floral Fortification: *Vesta's Hearth Offering*

The sign of Cancer is very much oriented toward love of home and family
as well as security. Mixed dried flowers, otherwise known as potpourri,
are now a popular household staple. It was a medieval custom to have
them in the house, revived by the Victorians. Use different combinations
for desired magical results; they help create sacred sanctuary space.

Gather together

- ⭑ 1 cup (20g) of dried rose petals
- ⭑ 1 cup (20g) of dried marigold
- ⭑ 1 cup (20g) of dried lily petals
- ⭑ a basket or bowl for the flower blend
- ⭑ clove essential oil
- ⭑ cinnamon essential oil

Timing: Either sun or moon in Cancer
is a perfect time for this offering to the
goddess of happy homes.

Put all the dried posies in the basket or bowl and sprinkle them with
the essential oils. Place the mixture on the south point of your altar
for the duration of a moon cycle. The sweet and spicy scent of the
potpourri will spread a positive and protective energy to your home
and your magical workings. A wreath of these same flowers with garlic
cloves added will protect you from harm and illness. If you are a
working witch, a small, sweet-smelling bowl of potpourri on your desk
will provide constant comfort. If you have a fireplace, keep some on
the mantle as an offering to the domestic goddess Vesta, she who
keeps the home fire burning. When the scent has faded, burn it in
your cast iron cauldron or a fireplace as an offering to her. Speak this
invocation when making the offering:

Vesta, goddess of home and hearth,
Stand guard over this place I love.
Keep safe the ones I love.
This night, we breathe in peace.
These flowers are my offering to you.
So mote it be.

Sanctuary Spell: *Rose-water Rite*

Three simple ingredients—a pink candle, a red rose, and water—can bestow a powerful steadying and calming influence. The rose signifies beauty, love for yourself and others, blossoming, budding, the earth, your heart, and peace. The candle stands for the yellow flame of the East, unity, harmony, focus, higher intention, and the light of the soul. Water is cleansing, free flowing, affects emotions, and stands for the West. This spell can be done alone or in a group where you pass the bowl around.

Timing: Sun or moon in Venus-ruled Libra is a sweet time to share this rite with those you care for.

Float a red rose in a clear bowl of water, and light a pink candle beside the rose. With the fingers of your left hand, gently stir the water and speak aloud this blessing:

I give myself life and health, refreshing water for my spirit.
I give myself time to rest, and space to grow.
I am love. My heart is as big as the world.
I am peace of mind. So be it, now and always.

Awaken the Imagination: *Age of Aquarius Spell*

Often, our state of mind grows restless when life becomes too routine.
Inspiration and imagination will remedy this instantly.

Gather together:

* ★ 1 green candle
* ★ 1 yellow candle
* ★ an amethyst crystal
* ★ a green apple
* ★ a small pine branch

Timing: Check your favorite celestial calendar to plan this spell for when the moon is in the sign of brilliance, Aquarius.

At one hour before midnight, place the two candles on your altar. Next to them, place the crystal, apple, and pine branch.

At 11:11 pm, hold the apple in the palm of your right hand and speak the following spell while circling the candlelit altar clockwise four times:

Sun and moon, awaken me tonight
With the power of Earth and Air, Fire and Water.
As I bite this fruit of knowledge, I am inspired.
All possibilities are before me. And so it is.

Eat the apple, then bury the seeds in your garden or in a potted plant. You will walk on a path new with promise of anything you can imagine. Keep the crystal and pine on your altar for as long as you wish and they will spark inspiration every time you see them.

Sensual Soak: *Scorpio Moon Rite*

Moon in Scorpio is the time to explore bodily pleasures. Sandalwood, amber, and vetiver are all rich, earthy scents that combine well together.

Gather together

★ 5 drops sandalwood essential oil

★ 5 drops amber essential oil

★ 2 drops vetiver essential oil

★ ½ cup (90g) Epsom salts

★ ½ cup (70g) baking soda

Combine the essential oils with the Epsom salts and stir in the baking soda. Mix well to create a richly scented paste. You can use a couple of different ways: either slather it onto yourself and shower off with a loofah and thick washcloth or, and this is my favorite way to soak up this earthly pleasure, roll it into a ball after you mix it and place under the faucet as you are running a hot bath. The entire room will smell like paradise. Soak it all in, lie back, and enjoy this fully.

If you want to keep this for the future or give as a thoughtful gift, you can store in a lidded container or roll into bath bombs and let them dry on wax paper or paper towels. This recipe can make three palm-size bath bombs. Note: you will be asked for more!

Embody the Goddess of Life: *Venus Rising Invocation*

Coconut milk creates a rich, moisturizing bath and leaves skin silky smooth. Ylang ylang is a heady, exotic scent that is lightened and heightened by the citrusy note of the orange.

Gather together

★ 2 drops ylang ylang essential oil

★ 3 drops orange essential oil

★ 1 can (14fl oz/400ml) of coconut milk

Timing: Both Venus-ruled Taurus and Libra sun and moon signs are very romantic, making them the perfect times for this goddess invocation.

Combine the essential oils with the coconut milk and add to a tubful of warm water.

Pray aloud to Venus:

Goddess of love and grace,
Bringer of all we so enjoy.
Fill both me and this space
With felicity, peace, and joy.
With harm to none, so mote it be.

Chapter 2

A Coven of One:

Solo Spells for the Solitary Practitioner

Our lives are basically a search for meaning. Creating and performing rites and spells on your own will help you define and strengthen your own identity and customize your desired outcome according to your individual will and intention. Performing rituals by yourself means you are your own priest or priestess, a solo seeker progressing along the spiritual path at your personal pace.

While group ritual (see Chapter 3) is about service, connection, and change, individual rites are powerful inner workings that kindle soul development and spiritual expansion. Group rituals are frequently tied to events, such as holidays, or a community crisis, such as an illness. Solitary ritual comes from your deepest inner rhythms. It comes from your own needs, your own questing, and your own psyche. With solitary rituals, you can also address private matters that you would rather not share with others or broadcast to the community.

Here is your opportunity to explore yourself through ritual. Ultimately, there will come a time when you need to design your own rituals as they spring up from the depths of your soul. Use the spells herein as examination of your deepest inner self.

Getting Grounded in Yourself: Chakra Centering Visualization

The best way to prepare for personal ritual is to center yourself. I call this "doing a readjustment," and I believe this is especially important in our overscheduled and busy world. Doing a readjustment helps pull you back into yourself and gets your priorities on track again. Only when you are truly centered can you do the genuine inner work of self-development that is at the core of ritual.

Centering takes many forms. Experiment on your own to find out what works best for you. My priestess pal Kat, for example, does a quick meditation that she calls "the chakra check-in." The chakra system comprises energy points in the astral body, an energetic aura attached to your physical body that is associated with various endocrine glands in the physical body. My friend closes her eyes and sits lotus-fashion (with her legs crossed, feet on thighs—but if you are on a bus or about to attend a meeting, you can do this centering exercise just sitting down, feet on the floor—and visualizes the light and color of each chakra. She brings to mind each chakra and mentally runs energy up and down her spine, from bottom to top, pausing at each chakra point. After she does this a few times, a soothing calm surrounds her. I have seen her perform her "chakra check-in" at trade shows and in hotel lobbies, surrounded by the hubbub of many people. She is an ocean of calm at the center of a storm. By working with your chakras, you can become much more in touch with your body and soul.

The *root chakra* is at the base of your spine and is associated with passion, survival and security, and the color red.

Above it is the *sacral chakra* in the abdominal region, which corresponds to such physical urges as hunger and sex, and the color orange.

The *solar plexus chakra* is associated with personal power, and the color yellow.

The *heart chakra* is the emotional center, for all strong feelings from love and happiness to the opposite. It is also associated with spiritual development, the higher self, and the color green.

The *throat chakra* is considered the center of communication, and is blue in color.

The *third eye chakra* is located in the center of your forehead and is associated with intuition, and the color indigo.

The *crown chakra* at the very top of your head is your connection to the universe, and is violet in color.

Prior to performing a ritual, try this centering exercise. Take a comfortable sitting position and find your pulse. Keep your fingers on your pulse until you feel the steady rhythm of your own heart. Now begin slowly breathing, in rhythm with your heartbeat. Inhale for four beats, hold for four beats, and then exhale for five beats. Repeat this pattern for six cycles. People have reported that although it seems hard to match up with the heartbeat at first, with a little bit of practice, your breath and heartbeat will synchronize. Your entire body will relax as you are filled with calm.

Crown Chakra Tonic for Insight

This magical hair tonic will clear your mind, awaken your senses, and open your crown chakra (the energy point at the top of your head), preparing the way for telepathic insight.

Gather together

★ 2-ounce (55ml) squeeze bottle

★ 4 drops rosewood essential oil

★ 2 tablespoons rosemary essential oil

★ a palmful of plain unscented hair conditioner

Timing: Ideally, perform this ritual when the sun or moon is in the truth-seeking signs of Gemini or Sagittarius for greatest effect.

Combine the oils and conditioner in the bottle. Shake well and pour onto your freshly shampooed hair while singing:

Sweetness, born of Rose,
Fly me on the wings of dreams.
We are made of sacred earth, purest water,
Sacred fire, wildest wind.
Blessing upon me. Blessing upon thee.
So mote it be.

At the very least, you will have visions and great clarity. You might even realize your true destiny. Wear your new wisdom gloriously, like a crown.

Guardians Circle Incantation

This little spell will take you far inside yourself. It will greatly empower you and instill in you a much deeper understanding of who you are and what you are here to do. Each of us is as individual as a snowflake, and our souls are imprinted with a stamp of specialness. The closer you get to the revelation of your soul's mission, the more you will know why you are here, and more importantly, what you are here to do. While the preparation takes a bit of time, the incantation is 5 minutes of pure magic.

Gather together

★ compass

★ 1 votive candle

★ pine essential oil

★ a 1 quart (1 liter) glass jar

★ incense

Timing: The best time to perform this spell is during the new moon, when the night sky is at its darkest.

Go outside and find a solitary space in which you can cast a circle. Use the compass to find true north. When you feel comfortable and safe to begin, cast a circle of energy in the center of the circle. Anoint your candle with the essence of pine, a tree that stays strong, green, and alive all through the winter. Place the candle in the glass jar and light it, setting both carefully and securely on the ground. Then light the incense with the flame of the candle and stick it into the ground beside the votive candle. Breathe slowly and deeply; make yourself mindful that you are here in the darkest night, celebrating the sacred. As you breathe, look at the majesty of nature and the world around you. Feel the ground beneath your feet. Listen to the silence that encompasses you. Now open your heart completely to the awesome power of the universe and the magic both inside and outside of you. Touch your third eye, the chakric place in the center of your forehead. With your eyes closed, speak aloud this rhyme:

Here beneath the moonless sky,
I open my heart and wonder why
I am here.
Tonight, I will learn
The reason why I yearn
To serve the Goddess and the God.
This night, I'll hear the reason
I serve this darkest winter season.
Guardians, I call on you now!

Remain at the center of the circle and keep your eyes closed. You may hear an inner voice, or you may hear an outer voice right beside your ear. Listen calmly, staying centered with your two feet on the ground. You will know when it is time for you to seal the circle and leave with your new message and mission. When you move, you will initiate the closing of the circle. Thank the guardians as you close the sacred space, being sure to leave everything exactly as you found it. Incense, jar, compass, candles, and matches all leave with you.

When you return home, write your message on a slip of paper and place it on your altar, where it will be hidden from any eyes but yours. Place the candle, jar, and any remaining incense on your altar and burn it for a few minutes each dark moon night.

Final thought: You may also want to begin a special journal of your thoughts, inspirations, and actions regarding the message you received. You have now embarked on an exciting new phase of your life's journey. Your journal will help you as you make discovery after discovery. Your journal may evolve into a Book of Shadows, or it may one day become a book like this!

Foretelling Your Future: *Mercury Sortilege*

The god Mercury prevails over communication, speed, prophecy, mental clarity, and fun. Traditionally, he also escorts the dead to the afterworld. All things yellow and citrus can bring forth Mercury's bright presence, which will help you in all your interactions with others. Try these surefire ways to make contact with the god of swiftness and time.

Gather together

* ☆ 3 yellow candles
* ☆ lemon essential oil
* ☆ neroli essential oil
* ☆ a notebook and a pen

Timing: It is best to do this during the waxing moon.

When the moon begins to wax, burn all three candles. Anoint yourself and the candles with the essential oils. Look at the flames and meditate upon them. Breathe deeply, filling your lungs with the fiery citrus scent. Holding both hands out, palms up, say:

Messenger of the gods,
Bring me your news.
Tonight, in this fire and flame,
Tell me the place and the name.
Mercury, messenger and god,
I will listen for your word on the wing.
Blessed be, to thee and me.

Now, you can either go to sleep with your dream journal nearby, or you can close your eyes and take up your pen for "automatic writing," allowing your hand and wrist to relax until you see what words take shape on the paper. Carefully record symbols and images that show up in your dreams; they all have meaning. Often, the names of people you will soon meet appear here first.

She Brings You Blessings and Strength:
Hecate Invocation

Hecate, above perhaps all others, is the original goddess of witchcraft. She is also the goddess of night, magic, necromancy, the moon, and ghosts. At "the witching hour of midnight," the power of magic is strongest. This is also the optimal time to call down the goddess known as "queen of the witches" for a power boost of blessings and strength. By honoring her and inviting her into your life, you will receive untold gifts of wisdom, joy, and beauty.

Gather together

* ✫ 1 large crystal, ideally a geode, amethyst, quartz, or rock crystal
* ✫ 3 candles in sturdy glass votives
* ✫ an image of the goddess
* ✫ a rattle or drum

Timing: The best time to perform this ritual is midnight.

Place the large crystal on your altar, along with candles and the goddess image.

Blessed one, all sky and earth and ocean is yours.
May we all be blessed by you.
May we all draw strength from you.
I sing to thee, bright lady.
I dance for thee, queen of all.
In your honor,
Blessed be.

Now, pick up your rattle or drum and shake or beat it while dancing under the midnight sky.

Your Unseen Helpers

The duties of the archangels are to serve God, assist humanity,
and watch and care for the lower ranks of angels.

The seven archangels and their associations are:

Raphael: healing

Gabriel: strength, personal guidance, and prophecy

Michael: protection and courage

Uriel: light

Ariel: wisdom

Cammuel: divine love

Cassiel: understanding

Writing to Archangel Michael for Protection

A study of angelic lore across the traditions indicates that the archangel
Michael is the oldest and most powerful of all angels, and as a personal
protector he can be called on or invoked when you need him for
courage, insight, spiritual growth, guidance, or in times of urgency.

There are many ways to call on the guidance of the angels. You can do this with a pendulum or meditation ritual; ask him to join you in a walk or in your dreams. In fact, in your dreams you will be much more open to receiving his messages. Before inviting Michael into your dream world, breathe deeply and achieve a state of total calm. Then think about why you feel the need for his guidance. Write down in your dream journal or Book of Shadows a specific invitation to him, such as,

"Michael, please come to me and help me to know if this potential new love (or new home or job, etc.) is right for me. Yes, you can and should be that specific. The clearer you are, the easier it is for the angel to provide aid. As you fall asleep, think about the circumstances and drift into your sleep and your dreams. The answer will be in your mind when you wake up. Write it down in the same journal and thank your angelic guest with a prayer of gratitude.

Rite for Welcoming Spirits

We can all use more benevolent energy in our lives. Some angels may take human form, such as a friend who is always there in a crisis. Others are hovering above in the ether and can be invoked with a few words and a focused intention. Use this spell when you need a guiding hand and angelic assistance.

Gather together

* 1 white and 1 blue candle (these are angelic hues)

* rosemary essential oil

* frankincense and myrrh incense

* celestite, a sky-blue crystal associated with angel energy (amethyst can substitute)

Anoint both candles with the rosemary essential oil. Light the white candle and use it to light the incense. If you were unable to acquire any frankincense or myrrh incense, you can use rosemary incense or light a rosemary branch in a fireproof glass or clay dish. Now light the blue candle with the white one and place them on either side of the crystal. Breathe deeply and speak this spell aloud to invoke the celestial guardians.

Guardians, I call upon you now
To bring aid and angelic blessings
By earth and sky, I invite you now
To point me to all that is good
And protect me from all that is not.
With gratitude to the heavenly host.
So mote it be.

Witch Craft: *Angel Accessing Charm for Protection*

In your travels along the sacred path, you doubtless have gathered up many natural treasures, such as seashells, driftwood, crystals, and small pebbles. You can create a simple "Angel Accessing Tool" from your collection of nature's blessings. Make an amulet any time you want to gather up the good energy of those unseen who can help and protect you (and drive away the not so helpful energy). Here's how to make an amulet you can hang whenever you need to call upon angelic aid.

Gather together

☆ sections of string, at least 6 inches (15cm) in length, one for each crystal

☆ small chunks of crystal (celestite, amethyst, aquamarine, muscovite, morganite, and selenite can all help you make contact with your guardian angels)

☆ a stick (a small piece of sea-smoothed driftwood is perfect)

Tie a piece of string around each chunk of crystal. Attach each string to your stick of wood so the crystals are hanging from the stick. Hang your amulet anywhere in your home you want to "make contact."

Once you have crafted your magical tool, you should store it in a safe place and bring it out when you really need angelic intervention. When I lived in a big city that had lots of car break-ins, I made one for my car and the era of broken windows ended for me. I recommend one for your office space, too. We all need work angels! You can welcome unseen and benevolent spirits into your home and life with this conjuring charm.

Incense Alchemy

Long ago, shamans and witches discovered that perfumed resins from herbs and tree branches could be thrown into the fire to release their properties. Ever since then, incense has been an essential tool in magical rites, recognized for its ability to restore universal equilibrium.

Making incense requires a mortar and pestle and a collection of 4-ounce (115ml) lidded jars. The incense is burned on small charcoal cakes, available at all metaphysical stores. Safe burning requires either a censor or use of a fireproof glass or clay dish.

Simple Incense Recipes

* *For peace of mind:* Crush sandalwood, bay leaves, and amber resin together. Burn a small amount on a charcoal cake in your fireproof glass or clay dish on your altar and meditate. The plant damania can be added to increase concentration.

* *For mastery of mind:* Crush together equal parts cinnamon and resinous benzoin. You will achieve your goals by burning this combination.

* *To enhance meditation:* Mix equal parts white sandalwood and frankincense, and add one-fourth part white orrisroot. Add a drop of oil from one of the following plants: angelica, agrimony, or aloe. Use this during the day of a full moon or during any lunar ceremony.

Herbal Helpers for Quick Protection Magic

You need look no further than your kitchen cabinet for other commonplace herbs to ward off unsettling energy:

* *Lemon rind:* Rubbed on furniture, doorjambs, and window frames, cleanses negative energy.

* *Rosemary:* When added to potpourri, woven into a wreath, or sprinkled on your doorstep, helps protect you.

* *Salt:* On the threshold of your home will keep away unwanted guests.

* *Kava kava:* Kava kava root guards against negative energy. Boil ground kava kava in a quart (1 liter) of water, let it cool and pour the water on your front step and walkway. To ramp the power up even more, add in 1 tablespoon each of ground cloves and cinnamon. Safety first!

Herbal Hex Breaker Ritual

Nothing can erode your inner calm more than being hexed or experiencing a run of bad luck and ill spirits. This foolproof spell requires you to obtain the bark of the wahoo plant from your herbalist. Known as *Euonymus atropurpureus*, it should never be ingested for any reason. Steep the bark in boiling water for 5 minutes. After it has cooled, dip your right index finger into the liquid and cross your forehead, saying seven times loudly, "Wahoo!" Whatever has been pestering you will leave your space immediately.

Invoking Your Inner Goddess: *Divine Essence Oil*

This relaxation remedy is an excellent way to create personal space after a hectic week.

Gather together

* ☆ 2 drops cedar essential oil
* ☆ 2 drops sandalwood essential oil
* ☆ 2 drops amber essential oil
* ☆ 2 drops lavender essential oil
* ☆ 4 drops carrier (or base) oil, such as sesame or jojoba
* ☆ a small bowl or vial, preferably heart-hued red

Timing: This tincture is most potent on goddess Freya's Day, Friday evening.

Mix together the essential oils with the carrier (or base) oil in the bowl or vial.

Touch one drop of the Divine Essence Oil on each pulse point: on both wrists, behind your ear lobes, on the base of your neck, and behind your knees. Wait a few moments and let the power of the goddess fill your senses as your mind, body, and spirit are renewed. Close your eyes and recite:

Freya, eternal and wise, give your strength to me now.
As I breathe, you are alive in me for this night.

Make sure to thank the goddess for all the blessings in your life.

Conjuring Cords

For ridding yourself of something (or someone) undesirable, try this spell.

Timing: Ideally this should be done during the waning moon.

Take 3 feet of string or fabric cord in banishing colors of gray or black. Begin tying knots as you chant:

By knot of one, my charms begun,
By two, my charms come true,
By knot of three, my desire is free.
By four, I shall have more.
By knot of five, I will thrive,
By six, ill fortune I nix.
By knot of seven, to Jove in heaven.
So mote it be.

Once you have finished, the string or cord should be given back to the earth by burying it in the ground or tossing it into a body of water, preferably a river.

Chapter 3

Rites of Passage:

Spells for Special Occasions, Birthdays, and Beyond

People often think of witchcraft as a solitary undertaking, best done between you and the moon. But the craft originally was nurtured and informed by groups of friends passing on herbal remedies, exchanging favorite plant seeds, and working rituals together in covens. Friends were also responsible for capturing the lore, spells, and healing arts of fellow witches and keeping the magic alive through the grand oral tradition of yore. Spellcraft was used to sow an especially fertile ground for family, friendships, marriages, and community. Witchcraft reflects the soul of humanity, celebrating the richness of the natural world around us and the beauty of the human heart.

On the wings of alliance, witchcraft flew and grew to be practiced worldwide. In its essence, Wicca is a wisdom tradition intended to aid our evolution, both individually and communally. It helps us maintain spiritual harmony with the earth and the stars, while also balancing our relationships with others.

Making Relationships Sacred: *Loved-one Shrine*

This sacred space is dedicated to the special people in your life: friends, family, and your partner. Your shrine can be a low table or even a shelf and provides a place to put gifts you have received from your loved ones, which might include crystals, jewelry, art, and lovely objects along with all their photos in frames. Every time I see my own special Loved-one Shrine, I smile. It fills my heart with love.

Gather together

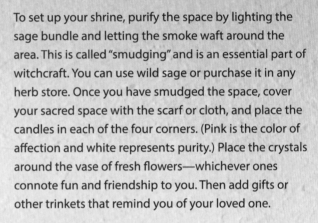

★ sage for smudging

★ a pink cloth or scarf

★ 2 pink candles and 2 white candles

★ a small rose quartz and fluorite crystals

★ a vase of fresh cut flowers of your choice (daisies, for example)

To set up your shrine, purify the space by lighting the sage bundle and letting the smoke waft around the area. This is called "smudging" and is an essential part of witchcraft. You can use wild sage or purchase it in any herb store. Once you have smudged the space, cover your sacred space with the scarf or cloth, and place the candles in each of the four corners. (Pink is the color of affection and white represents purity.) Place the crystals around the vase of fresh flowers—whichever ones connote fun and friendship to you. Then add gifts or other trinkets that remind you of your loved one.

Light the candles, kneel before your newly created shine and say:

I light the fire of loyalty
The heat of heart and the flame of love
and friendship.
Brightest blessing, Great Goddess bring,
The spirit of friendship will surely sing.
As the fates do dance, I welcome the chance
To share my love and my life.
So mote it be.

The Flame of Friendship

You can further charge the candles on your Loved-one Shrine by scratching your desire into the wax. I use the thorn of a rose for this and write the words of my intention. Many witches use symbols: a moon, the sun, a flower, a heart, a dollar sign, or a number, for example. You can also inscribe a name.

Take a large solar-hued yellow pillar candle anointed with lemon or bergamot essential oil and charge it with positivity toward your loved ones. Scratch your own name into it and write "I love ____" with the name of your friend or family member.

Light the candle and say four times:

I love me. I love _____.

For a daily dose of one-minute magic, light the candle every night and repeat this love charge before bed and every morning when you arise. Your heart will lift and soar, which then emanates outward toward this special person in your life.

A Celestial Guide to Companionship

I rely upon my knowledge of astrology to inform me whether a new acquaintance has the potential to become a dear friend (or more). While the elements of Earth, Air, Fire, and Water are a major indicator of compatibility (Earth signs naturally get along with other Earth signs, for example), you should endeavor to have your astrological charts done and compare them. Finding the sun and the moon in the same sign is common among many soul mates. This is known as synastry in astrology. As example, a man with a Virgo sun will be attracted to a woman with a Virgo moon and this is true for every sun and moon combination. It is a true affinity.

* *Fire signs:* Leo, Sagittarius, and Aries. People with these signs are bold, courageous, and fun-loving, and they play well together.

* *Water signs:* Cancer, Scorpio, and Pisces. These mysterious folks are sensitive, passionate, and creative, and they comfortably swim in the same current.

* *Air signs:* Gemini, Libra, and Aquarius. These smart, talkative, and artistic people speak the same language.

* *Earth signs:* Taurus, Virgo, and Capricorn. These practical, savvy, and successful types enjoy helping each other to the top.

* If you are born on one of the "cusp" days, then consider it a blessing. You get along with everybody!

Coven Welcoming Ceremony

In your witchy community, a new name is an important signifier. It is a marker of your initiation and progress on your pagan path, and it lets the world know your intention and identity. When you are ready to take this step or induct a new witch into your community or coven, this ritual is a beautiful way to mark the occasion ceremoniously. Ideally, the high priestess or leader selects the name, but we witches can also choose what expresses our spirituality best. The greeting and welcoming of the newly named coven member is 5 minutes of pure magic.

Gather together

* firewood and kindling

* a sage wand for blessing with smoke

* "gifts of wisdom" for the newly ordained witch

* drums

Timing: This ritual is best performed on the night of the new moon.

Gather together the tribe, start the fire, and form a seated circle around the flames. Pass the sage wand around for the blessing of smoke.

Present the new name with the explanation of the name. For example, "I greet you 'Lady Silverlake,' so named because you are brilliant and reflective; because you shine."

The group should welcome the newly christened witch by going around the circle and speaking their blessings and hopes for the new pagan's future. "Lady Silverlake, may you see the world and find the place that speaks most deeply to your heart."

Next, the group should present the newly named tribal member with the gifts of wisdom. We are not speaking here of pricey prizes but perhaps a book that changed your life and the reason why, or an amber amulet for protection.

Drum and sing on this new-moon night, as an important new member of the tribe has just come into being!

Your Personal New Year: *Birthday Rite*

The anniversary of your birth is like a new year, when everyone can start again, wearing new clothes, beginning life anew with a fresh attitude and bright hopes. Invite your friends and loved ones over for this special day.

Gather together

- ★ plenty of candles
- ★ 1 cup (240ml) of water
- ★ a dish of salt
- ★ incense
- ★ a new piece of clothing (such as a scarf) or a new item of jewelry
- ★ a plate of cakes and sweets to share

Light as many candles as you can in the room where you are performing this ritual. Create a circle of candles, and create a sacred space by having a symbol of each element in your circle: a dish of salt for Earth, a cup of water, incense for Air, and a candle for Fire. Sit lotus-style in the center of your circle and relax in the flickering candlelight. Feel the presence of the four elements and the balance they create. Notice how warm and alive the room feels. Notice how the gentle, flickering candlelight makes all feel safe. As you bask in the atmosphere of the loving candlelight, say to each of your guests, one by one:

I am grateful to have you in my life. May the power of Earth, Air, Fire, and Water bless you.

When you have finished your statements of appreciation, purify the new piece of clothing or item of jewelry by passing it through the smoke of the incense. Then put on your new piece of jewelry or clothing, saying:

With this act, I declare this new year is here, and see the future bright with hope.

Stay within your circle of light for 5 minutes. Then share the food and libations and relax with your special friends. Leave some of the cake or sweets as an offering to the gods in thanks for your new life in the coming solar year.

A Home for the New Soul: *Baby Blessing*

If any ritual is meant to be swift, it is the blessing of a new baby into the family and tribe. The baby will often quite vocally let everyone know when time is up and even that just adds to the fun!

Gather together

★ a bright blue cloth for swaddling

★ a vial of water that has been blessed

You don't need any other supplies, just loving, happy people with the new parents and their child. A priestess or elder conducts the ceremony and begins by welcoming all and speaking a personal intention for the new parents and the baby. She then carefully swaddles the baby in the blue cloth and begins singing this song:

We all come from the Goddess
And to her we shall return
Like a drop of water,
Flowing to the ocean.

As below, so above.
Mother, father, daughter, son,
Wisdom's gift shall be your own.
Crone and sage, youth and sage
We welcome you with all our hearts of love.

Gently pour a drop of the blessed water on the baby's head and chant the blessing again.

At this point, the little one will doubtless be ready for a nap and the tribe should go for a joyful feast.

Predictions for the New Year: *Divination Conjuration*

Gather a group of women together around a large table you can use as the altar. Ask them to bring feast books to share and offerings of fruit, flowers, or vegetables as altar offerings to the Goddess.

Gather together

* 13 candles

* a black bowl filled with water

Timing: January 1.

Place the offerings and the 13 candles on the altar around the bowl filled with water, which is to be used as a scrying mirror (to foretell the future). Light the candles and turn down the lights and say aloud:

Fruit, flower, and Goddess's herb,
Perform for me enchantment superb.
You give us grain and bread.
Foretell for me the year ahead.

After placing the offerings on the altar, one at a time, each woman should kneel over the mirror and look upon the water. Some people may see images, but oftentimes the information comes as an impression, a thought, or meditative reflection. People should only share their visions if they feel the need to do so.

After each woman has had a turn, everyone should chant and sing together:

Daughters under this sun
Sisters under this moon
Tonight we receive your blessings
Goddess great and good—
We thank you for the year to come.

An Enchanted Engagement

When two people in love decide to get married, it is a wonderful event for the entire community of friends and family. It is good to toast the happy couple and acknowledge this momentous occasion. Invite them over and anyone else who may want to share in this blessing.

Gather together

★ yellow roses and yellow candles to symbolize joy

★ champagne and sparkling cider and flutes for serving

★ sweet cakes and cookies, round in shape to symbolize rings

Once everyone has arrived, light the candles and hand one rose to each of the betrothed. Speak this blessing:

Today we share our love with both of you
We share in your joy for the future.
You have given your hearts to each other
We give our hearts to you.
We celebrate this bright beginning
And all the happiness it will bring.
Blessed be, dear ____ and ____ [speak the names of the couple]
You will give and live in total joy.
Blessed be to thee. So mote it be!

Now pop the champagne and pass the bottle and the sweets around and share in this loving toast.

The Crown of Cronehood: *A Ritual of Honoring*

Women should feel good about aging. They should celebrate long, full lives, and be respected and honored for the wisdom they bring to the community. Croning rituals, such as this one, are the signal to the group that a woman has ascended into a new role of service and leadership to the family, the tribe, the village, and the sisterhood. Elders say this coming of age occurs at the woman's second Saturn return, which is at age 58 to 60, but modern women now often decide for themselves.

While this ritual can last as long as is needed, the actual crowning lasts for 5 very magical minutes.

Gather together

* a flowering branch
* a crown or tiara (you can easily obtain one at any costume shop), placed on the altar table
* enough candles to represent every year of the crone's life

Upon the arrival of the soon-to-be-crowned crone, the eldest woman present should take a flowering branch, dip it in water, and sprinkle it on the crone's head, just a few drops, and speak this blessing:

I bless you in the name of the Goddess.
I bless you in the name of Mother Earth.
I bless you in the name of every woman.
Sister, do you accept the role of teacher and leader as crone?

The crone responds. If she accepts the title, then the eldest woman says:

She is crowned.

The eldest woman places the Crown of Cronehood upon the new crone's head. Now everyone should speak together:

We gather together to celebrate that [new crone's name] is entering the Wise Age.

Now the eldest woman and the youngest woman present light the candles. After everyone has spoken her tribute to the crone, she can speak her thanks. When the newly crowned crone has spoken from her heart, she ends with "Blessed be to all." Food is then served, and it should be a birthday party to remember for a lifetime.

Goddess Visualization: *Group Guided Meditation*

I have led many groups in this guided meditation. Everyone should gather in a circle and make themselves very comfortable, sitting on the ground, standing, or even lying down. All you need to bring is an open mind and a pen and paper to record the special message Mother Goddess has for you.

Blessed beings, you are about to enter the Mother, our great earth Goddess, Gaia. In your mind, you are standing with bare feet on the ground. You can feel the grass with your toes, the solid earth underneath your feet. Feel the solidity and power of the earth as it fills your body with strength; we are all made of clay. We come from her, and we are made of earth. Feel your connection to the Mother. We are made of stardust and clay and the waters of the ocean. Feel the blood in your veins. The water of life. Know that you are alive. Feel her winds, the breath of life. Breathe deeply ten times, completely filling your lungs and completely emptying your lungs. Breathe and feel your chest rising and falling with each breath.

Now feel your backbone connecting to the earth; you feel a cord connecting you and your life to the earth. Concentrate on the cord until you can feel it running all the way through you and deep into the earth. Tug on the cord; feel it give. Now, take the cord in your hands and follow it down, down deep into the earth. It is dark as you go down and down, but do not be frightened. Trust in the universe and keep descending into the bosom of the Mother. Down we go, not falling but moving purposefully, gracefully, following the cord of the earth. Now you see light. Keep moving toward the light and keep holding the cord as it leads you to the shining distance.

The light grows nearer, and you see that it is an opening, a cave, a safe place in which to shelter. Enter the cave. It is filled with light, firelight reflected off a thousand crystal points. An old woman sits at the fire, warming her bones in her cozy dry cave. It is beautiful, more beautiful than the palace of any king or the castle of any queen. It is the crystal cave of the Goddess, and you are with her. Show your respect to the Goddess and light the incense at her altar at the side of the cave, piled up with many shimmering stones and priceless gems, the bounty and beauty of our generous benefactor.

Sit quietly and heed the special message she has for you. You are her child, and she has dreamed a dream for you. Now we listen and breathe. Blessed be.

Now open the circle and sit in silence for a moment, so that everyone present can record her impressions and visions in a journal. In years to come, if you and your circle of women decide to observe this rite annually, as I recommend, you can share and compare notes from prior years. This is a wonderful way to process the passages of your lives.

Happy Ever After Housewarming

When you have settled into your new home, invite your friends and family over to bless the rooms and ensure that you are surrounded with good energy.

Timing: The optimal time for a housewarming is during the new moon.

Take a bowl or cup of water and add a sprinkle of salt. Stand in the front room, near the front door. Dip your fingers in the water and sprinkle droplets on the threshold. Now turn to the east and say:

Powers of the East,
Source of the sun rising,
Bring hope and inspiration.

Sprinkle some water in the east, then turn to the south and say:

Powers of the South,
Source of summer's warmth and light,
Bring joy and bounty.

Sprinkle some water in the south, then turn to the west and say:

Powers of the West,
Source of oceans and rivers,
Bring the power of the waves.

Sprinkle some water in the west, then turn to the north and say:

Powers of the North,
Source of the winter, place of the mountains, and the polestar,
Bring security and sight.

Now bring out the wine, mead, and sparkling cider and celebrate because you have now blessed this house!

Chapter 4

Healing in a Hurry:

Herbs, Teas, and Curatives for You and Your Family

Healing spells are "earth magic." The rituals that create both soundness of body and clarity of mind are eminently practical. They are a wonderful mix of gardening, herb lore, minding the moon and sky, and heeding ancient folk wisdom. Healing magic uses enchantments in conjunction with the properties of herbs and plants—a powerful combination. It is a subtle process, growing more effective over time through repeated practice. A modern witch knows that most maladies come from myriad causes, with such common roots as neglect, imbalance, high stress, and lack of sleep, which includes eating the wrong types of foods. A good witch knows that prevention is always better than a cure, and spellcraft can greatly assist the body's powerful self-healing properties.

Healing magic is, of course, about far more than the spoken words of spells. The greater the clarity of intention and concentration you bring to bear, the more powerful your conjuring will be. Before you begin using any of the spells contained herein, think about the words and your intention, gathering energy from a place deep within. You will also need a strong "home base," a source of inspiration and strength that is centered at your altar. Lavish energy on a well-wrought altar, and you will gain results tenfold.

Kitchen Witchery Cures: Remedy Recipes

Many remedies can be made from what you have in the kitchen, from spices as well as herbs and plants. Here are a few simple tried-and-tested recipes handed down through generations of wise women:

* *Nutmeg Milk:* Grated nutmeg soothes heartburn, nausea, and upset tummies. Use a grater to grate a small amount (about ⅛ teaspoon) to 1 mug of warmed milk (cow, soy, rice, or oat milk). It is comforting and curing.

* *Cayenne Infusion:* Use this pepper as a remedy for colds, coughs, sore throats, heartburn, hemorrhoids, and varicose veins, or as a digestive stimulant and to improve circulation. Make an infusion by adding ½ teaspoon cayenne powder to 1 cup (240ml) boiled water. Add 2 cups (480ml) of hot water to make a more pleasant and palatable infusion. Add lemon and honey to taste.

* *Catnip by the Cup:* This herb is not just for kitties! We humans can also benefit from it as a remedy for upset tummies as well as a way to diminish worry, anxiety, and nervous tension. Take a palmful of dried catnip leaves and steep in a cup (240ml) of boiling water for 5 minutes. Strain as you would any loose tea. Honey helps even more and a cup or two of catnip tea per day will have you in fine fettle, relaxed and ready.

* *Cranberry Cure:* How many times did your mom tell you to drink your cranberry juice? Turns out she was right to insist. Unsweetened cranberry juice is very good for bladder health and also benefits men as it's great for prostate health, too. Two half cups (two lots of 120ml) a day, mom's orders!

* *Echinacea Root:* Every herb store or organic grocer will have dried echinacea root for fighting colds and negating respiratory infections. It is an amazing immune booster! Just mince a teaspoonful and steep in a cup (240ml) of boiling water. Sweeten to taste and drink at least a couple of cups a day.

Other Herbs for Medicinal Teas

You can use the basic recipe of steeping a palmful of herbs for 5 minutes in a cup (240ml) of boiling water and use these plants either fresh or dried:

* *Lemon balm* is a true aid for insomnia, anxiety, and restlessness.

* *Licorice root* is marvelous for stomach and mouth ulcers.

* *Marshmallow,* both root and leaf, strengthens the gastrointestinal tract and your mucus membranes.

* *Milk thistle* is excellent for your liver and kidneys.

* *Mullein leaves* help sore throats, coughs, and chest congestion.

* *Nettle,* either fresh or dried, prevents allergies.

* *Slippery elm bark* will get rid of heartburn, a bad cough, and a sore throat.

* *St John's Wort* extract is good for depression, PMS, and hot flashes.

* *Thyme* is trusted to help with colds and congestion and is an antispasmodic.

A Cup Brimming with Health: *Vitamin C Tea*

This tonic provides bioflavonoids and vitamin C in an organic, natural way so all the nutrients are easily available for absorption. Drink this blend regularly and you will feel fantastic. The amounts of ingredients are given in parts, as you may want to make a big batch of tea for the whole family.

Gather together

* ☆ 2 parts lemongrass
* ☆ 3 parts hibiscus
* ☆ 4 parts rose hips
* ☆ 1 part chopped cinnamon sticks
* ☆ a teapot
* ☆ honey

Blend the herbs using your mortar and pestle. Place in a teapot with 4 cups (960ml) of hot water. Steep for 5 minutes in your teapot, then strain and serve sweetened with honey to taste. If you make ahead, you should keep the mixed herbs in an airtight container. Serve regularly as a preventative during cold and flu season.

Quick Tips:
Black, Green, and White Tea

Use black tea for an upset tummy and headache. Green tea strengthens the immune system, and you can reuse tea bags to stanch cuts or calm insect bites. White tea, green tea, and black tea are all made from the leaves of *Camellia sinensis*. White tea is made from the youngest leaves of the plant; it is a sweet brew and has less caffeine than green or black tea. It is also rich in antioxidants and is recommended for reducing "bad" cholesterol and improving artery health. White tea is a little costly, but a good choice for health and flavor.

First Aid Aromatherapy: Essential Oil Magic

Blending essential oils for magic is both an art and a science. Combining these herbal oils can take their individual properties to the next level, interacting together to perform curative miracles.

Classic Essential Oils

* One drop of *lavender* essential oil warmed between the palms of your hands can summon an instant sense of serenity.

* One whiff of *bergamot* essential oil can calm anxiety and stimulate the mind.

* *Ylang ylang* essential oil can combat hypertension.

* *Rosemary* essential oil kindles the memory and can help with perspiration.

A great blend involves combining notes—typically a top, middle, and base, though some blends don't require a base—to create a balanced and effective aroma.

The top note is the first scent impression, which gives way to the middle note—the star of the show. The base note gives the blend its staying power and usually comes to the forefront much later. The aim in blending these three notes is to create a ratio that results in a harmonious cocktail that works (olfactorily or topically, depending on the blend) to address specific moods or ailments. A good rule of thumb is to use approximately 30 percent top note, 50 percent middle, and 20 percent base. If the blend doesn't require a base note, round it up to about 40 percent top and 60 percent middle. Always use the highest-quality organic essential oils (see Resources, page 141) for the best outcomes. Consult your local herbal apothecary and look for brands that have had GC/MS testing as that is known as the gold standard test for essential oils. I keep a stock of ½-ounce (15ml) dark-colored vials with stopper lids and blank labels for when aromatherapy needs arise.

For the following blends, carefully pour the oils into a vial and shake gently to blend. You can rub this on pulse points or use a diffuser. These are quite popular. If you are using a diffuser, no carrier (or base) oil is needed. I use the simplest and most old-fashioned kind of diffuser, which is a clay ring you can put at the base of a light bulb in a lamp. The warmth of the bulb slowly fills the space with the desired scent and effect. If you plan to use your blend on pulse points, you will need a carrier oil. Always do a skin test first to avoid any potential irritation.

Jubilant

The sweet scent of this blend makes you feel all warm and fuzzy—euphoric, even.

* 1 drop each of top notes: bergamot, lemon, neroli

* 1 drop each of middle notes: ylang ylang, jasmine, Roman chamomile, geranium, rose

* 1 tablespoon of a carrier (or base) oil, ideally jojoba or apricot

Quietude

If you need a moment of peace, try this citrus-floral blend.

* 3 drops of top note: orange

* 5 drops of middle note: ylang ylang

* 2 drops of base note: patchouli

* 1 teaspoon carrier (or base) oil, ideally sesame or jojoba

Bright Mind

Clear the mind and gain a keen sense of alertness with this bright, sunny blend.

* 1 drop each of top notes: rosemary, peppermint, bergamot, lemon

* 1 drop each of middle notes: mint, geranium, ylang ylang, jasmine, Roman chamomile

* 1 teaspoon carrier (or base) oil, almond or grapeseed

Calm Emotion Potion

Why does every day seem like it is as long as a week nowadays? Unplugging from cable news and constant social media feeds will help, as will this time-tested aromatherapy healing potion. This remedy is an excellent way to recharge and refresh after a hectic week.

Gather together

* ☆ a small ceramic or glass bowl
* ☆ 2 drops bergamot essential oil
* ☆ 2 drops vanilla essential oil
* ☆ 1 drop amber essential oil
* ☆ 2 drops lavender essential oil
* ☆ 4 drops carrier (or base) oil, apricot or sesame, ideally

Timing: This tincture is most potent right after the sun sets, by the light of the moon.

Mix all the oils together in the bowl.

Take off your shoes so you can be more grounded. Walk outside, and stand on your veranda or by an open window. Now, close your eyes, lift your head to the moon, and recite aloud:

Bright moon goddess, eternal and wise, give your strength to me now.
As I breathe, you are alive in me for this night.
Health to all, calm to me.
So mote it be.

Gently rub one drop of Calm Emotion Potion on each pulse point: on both wrists, behind your ear lobes, on the base of your neck, and behind your knees. Close your eyes and breathe the sweetly serene scent in as you stand barefoot for 5 full minutes. If you need more time to restore yourself and regain your calm, continue your mindful breathing and contemplation. As the oil surrounds you with its warm scent, you will be filled with a quiet strength.

Waters of Wellness

For thousands of years, we humans have been "taking the waters" as a way to restore, and also heal illness. A ritual bath that will simultaneously relax and stimulate you, is a rare and wonderful thing.

Gather together

- ★ 4 cups (720g) of Epsom salts
- ★ a large glass bowl
- ★ ½ cup (120ml) of almond carrier (or base) oil
- ★ 6 drops comfrey essential oil
- ★ 4 drops eucalyptus essential oil
- ★ 4 drop rosemary essential oil;
- ★ 6 drops bergamot essential oil

Pour the salts into the bowl and fold in the carrier (or base) oil. Now add in the essential oils, stirring after each is added. Continue to blend the mixture until it is moistened thoroughly. You can add more almond oil if necessary.

When your bath tub is one-quarter full, add one-quarter of the salt mixture under the faucet. Breathe in deeply ten times, inhaling and exhaling fully before you recite this:

Healing spirits I offer myself to you.
Remove from me any impurities
Of the spirit and mind, I open myself to you,
Body, heart, and soul.
With harm to none and healing to me, so mote it be.

When the tub is full, step inside and exercise your breath ten more times. Repeat the prayer while you use the rest of the salts to scrub your body, carefully avoiding your eye area. Rest and rejuvenate as long as you like while visualizing your renewed health and vigor.

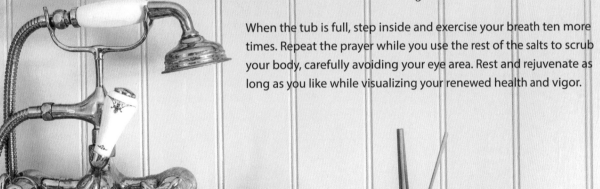

Cast Out All Ills: *Floor Cleanser*

Commercial cleansers are chock full of chemicals and potential toxins so
I urge you to rethink using them. Simple herbal DIY cleaners are much
healthier for you and your loved ones and always smell more natural.
Who doesn't love the smell of lavender, citrus, and fresh mint?

Gather together

* a ceramic bowl
* hot water
* 1 quart (1 liter) of white vinegar
* 2 limes
* 2 lemons
* a handful of fresh mint
* 6 drops lavender essential oil
* a bucket
* a clean mop

In a ceramic bowl, pour 2 cups (480ml) of hot water and half a cup (120ml) of lime and lemon juice, then add the fresh mint leaves and the lavender oil. Stir and let steep for a half hour, then strain out the leaves and compost them.

Take a clean bucket and fill it with two gallons of warm water, then pour in the essential oil mixture. Dip your mop into the bucket, wring it out, and clean the floor very thoroughly. Chant this charm as you use the mop:

Nothing but health and happiness here
Brightness and joy only remain in this sphere.
Anything dark and ill, I cast you out!
Harm to none, blessing throughout.

Awakened Breath Incantation

Unless you are already a practitioner of magical arts, you may well be casting
spells unconsciously that throw obstacles in your path. Negative thoughts can
imprint and start to manifest in an unfortunate way.

To clear the way to greater wealth and happiness, go for a walk during the next new moon. Pick up a white stone or white flower and place it on your altar. Light a white candle, and then close your eyes. Empty your mind and breathe deeply. Check to make sure your mind is not wandering; if any negative thoughts are lingering, send them out of your mind permanently.

After ten deep inhales and exhales, you should begin to feel a buzzing at the crown of your head. Now, open your eyes stare into the flame of the candle and repeat seven times:

I am alive.
I have power
It is real
And so it is.

Any time you find yourself engaged in negative self-talk or thinking, repeat this spell.

Mineral Medicine

Since the dawn of human kind, people have carried stones and crystals as helpers and as talismans; for protection and good luck. In so doing, they have brought themselves a greater sense of security. For peace of mind, the strongest "medicine" consists of an amethyst, a rhodochrosite, and a turquoise. While they may sound exotic, they are commonly available in metaphysical stores. (We will find out more about the power of crystals in Chapter 7.)

Gather together

* a small sky-blue bag

* an amethyst crystal

* a rhodochrosite crystal

* a turquoise crystal

Place the crystals in the bag. When you are ready, hold the pouch in your hand and incant:

Stones of the earth,
warmed by the sun,
Clear away trouble,
Help and healing is now begun.

I recommend leaving your pouch on your altar where it can be at the ready whenever needed.

Awesome Altar Stones

Crystals are finally being acknowledged for their power to give greater physical strength and health, and can be added to your healing altar (see page 76). *Turquoise* stones are grounding, and *agates* raise the energy level. For good circulation, try *carnelian*. For keeping life on an even keel, the organic gem family— *shells*, *corals*, and *abalone*—is optimal. For impetus and motivation, work with *carnelian*. To boost your health and well-being, try *red coral* for the lungs, *bloodstone* for the heart, and *moonstone* during pregnancy.

Quick Tips:
Instant Inspiration

* To lift your spirits, light a green candle and hold harmony-bringing *jade* while meditating.

* Carrying a *quartz* crystal will create tranquility inside and around you.

* If you're feeling overwhelmed or under duress, hold *black obsidian*. If the stress is caused by an overabundant workload, keep the obsidian on your desk. Obsidian absorbs the negative.

The Goddess of Healing: *Artemis Invocation*

Creating a healing altar will safeguard your physical health and that of your loved ones. Your altar is your sacred workspace. It is charged with your personal power. Set up your healing altar facing north, the direction associated with the energy of manifestation. North is also the direction of the hour of midnight, the "witching hour," and an altar set up facing north at midnight promises potent magic. Your shrine to the healing craft should be highly personal and represent all that signifies wellness to you.

This altar is dedicated to the goddess Artemis (see right).

Gather together

* ☆ white fabric
* ☆ 2 green candles, for health, in green glass holders or votive glasses
* ☆ a small statue of Artemis, or a moon-shaped symbol to represent her
* ☆ incense such as sandalwood, camphor, or frankincense
* ☆ healing crystals and objects that bring comfort

To ensure healthful beginnings, drape the white fabric over your altar to make a tabula rasa, or altar equivalent to a blank slate. Take the candles and position them in the two farthest corners of the altar. Place the Artemis statue at the center of the altar. Place an incense burner between the two candles and light the incense.

Now adorn your altar with objects that symbolize healing energy to you. You may perhaps choose a candleholder carved from a chunk of amethyst crystal, which contains healing properties; an abalone shell with the iridescent magic of the oceans; a sweet-smelling bundle of sage; a small citrus plant bursting with the restorative power of vitamins; or a bowl of curative salts from the sea.

These symbolic items, and any others that you select, will energize your altar with the magic that lives inside you. It is also important that the altar be pleasing to your eye and makes you feel good when you look at it so that you want to spend time there each and every day. After you have been performing rituals there for a while, a positive healing energy field will radiate from your altar.

Artemis, Goddess of the Healing Moon

Artemis is one of the best-known goddesses and, as it turns out, is one of the most needed as she is a healing divinity. She is the Greek goddess of the moon. In her Roman form, Diana, she is the deity to whom Dianic witches and priestesses are devoted. She is a bringer of luck, the goddess of the hunt, and a powerful deity for magic and spellwork. As the huntress, she can help you search out anything you are looking for, whether it is tangible or intangible. As a lunar deity, she can illuminate you. Invoke Artemis when you want to practice moon magic, by saying aloud "I call upon you, beloved Artemis." I suggest you study her mythology further to design original lunar ceremonies. Enshrine her by dedicating an altar or sacred space to her to bring about any of her marvelous qualities and to bring about healing.

Quick Tip:
Earring Alleviation
Wear one gold earring and one silver earring to rid yourself of the discomfort of a headache.

Chapter 5

Prompt Prosperity:

Money Magic Secrets for True Abundance

For centuries, witches have known that luck is neither random nor mysterious. Thanks to the wise women in my family who shared their "trade secrets" openly, I learned very early in life that I could manifest my will through the tools of magic. When in a pinch, I have used witchcraft to replenish the coffers. I have also used prosperity spells to find a good home, attract job opportunities, and help others.

When I arrived penniless in San Francisco after graduate school, and realized that rent was ten times more expensive than my pocket could bear, my friends were impressed when I got a job at a prestigious stockbrokerage firm on my first day job hunting, and found a spacious Victorian apartment (complete with a witchy cupola) just a few days later. None of this was accidental, I assure you.

As soon as you approach your prosperity consciously, you will see that you have the power to choose abundance. And when you increase your material prosperity, you reduce the need to worry about such worldly matters or about just getting by, day to day. Then you can move on to achieving true prosperity: expanding your mind through learning, pursuing your pleasures, spending time with family and friends, and enjoying your life.

Pointing the Way to Prosperity

For prosperity spells, I recommend having a wand made from ash (*Fraxinus excelsior*). Ash grows fast and its seedlings root everywhere, so it's persistent. Use ash for prosperity and self-improvement.

If your prosperity wand can fit well on your altar, I suggest keeping it there and you can also use a crystal at the end, such as citrine (see page 114) to boost the power of any ritual you are working on your altar. For example, whatever ritual elements symbolize money, point your wand with its crystal at those for an extra charge.

Money Flow: *Feng Shui Fountain*

Water fountains are good feng shui and can enhance your prosperity quotient. For those of us who can't pull off a fountain in our home or garden, this works just as well to get the money flowing.

Gather together

☆ at least 8 small, smooth river rocks

☆ a large green bowl or tall vase

☆ enough water to fill the container

☆ your prosperity wand

Stand in the front door area of your home and identify which is the far-left corner. This is the prosperity area and, therefore, the perfect place for this ritual. Place the smooth river rocks in the bottom of the bowl or vase and carefully pour in the water so you avoid spilling any. Take up your wand and speak aloud:

In the name of the Goddess, I dedicate this space.
Peace and prosperity flows throughout this place.
Everyone here will enjoy abundance and grace.
With harm to none. So mote it be.

Gently stir the surface of the water with your wand so it swirls and circles. Repeat the spell, then bow and say thank you to the energies of abundance.

Remove the stones from the vessel and pour the water onto the roots of the nearest tree or one of your larger potted plants, ideally right outside your home. Keep the stones in the far left corner of your home for continual good feng shui. This will keep the flow of abundance in your personal space.

Prosperity Pouches: *DIY Charm Bags*

A charm bag is a little bag or pouch filled with objects charged with magic for a specific intent. You can charge the objects with magic by placing them on your altar for 24 hours or, for a 5-minute fix, use spellwork, as suggested here.

Gather together

* ✪ 12 inches (30cm) green cord or string
* ✪ 1 green candle
* ✪ thyme or cinnamon incense
* ✪ a small muslin or cloth bag/pouch (that could fit in the palm of your hand)
* ✪ bolline
* ✪ 1 cinnamon stick
* ✪ 1 teaspoon dried basil leaves
* ✪ 3 pebble-size crystals of green jade, peridot, or turquoise

Set the cord or string aside and place all the other items on your altar. Stand at your altar and light the candle and incense. Pick up the pouch and smudge it in the sweet smoke of the incense while saying the following spell:

My life is blessed and this I know.
Into this bag, prosperity will flow.
I see the future is bright wherever I go,
My life is blessed; this much I know.
With harm to none; so mote it be.

Using your bolline, cut the cinnamon stick into 3 pieces. Cut the green cord or string into 3 pieces. Place the basil, crystals, and cinnamon into the pouch. Now take the pieces of green cord and, one at a time, tie the end of the bag securely. Keep it with you in your pocket and into your life, money will flow.

Prosperity Intention

I had a very scary financial situation in 2008, right before the "credit crunch," which became known as The Great Recession. I had moved in with my fiancé and we bought a home together at the very edge of San Francisco with a teeny Pacific Ocean view. He worked in tech and his earnings were much more than mine but we never gave it a second thought. It was a modest home but we loved it and I threw myself into gardening, sowing herb beds, arranging sacred shrines and all the lovely aspects of Wiccan nesting.

He passed away unexpectedly before our marriage and before the shock of that even subsided, I was hit with bills for funeral arrangements, house payments, hospital bills, and myriad unforeseen expenses that left me close to broke and going underwater on the mortgage. I was deep in grief but knew I had to get myself out. I needed to sell the house as quickly as possible, find an affordable place to rent in the San Francisco Bay Area, pack up and move and also earn more money.

In times like these, group magic is called for. I asked a group of girlfriends who had been very supportive during all the travails if they would meet with me once a week for Intending. They were happy to help and curious, too. The first time we met, we all set an intention for a desired outcome or need—I couldn't help but notice that all their intentions were more achievable than mine—and brought potluck food to share.

We began our group ritual by going round the circle and stating our gratitude for all we do have in our lives.

Next we each set our intention regarding our desired need or outcome. Kara said, "I need a free bookcase for my baby's books and toys. I ask this for the good of all. And so it is."

Our circle was a small and loving group of five women so it took less than 5 minutes for us to set our individual intentions. Afterward, I spoke my deep thanks for their support and we shared the food.

The next morning, I got a call from Kara. She said, "You are not going to believe this but I walked outside of our apartment building and there was a bookcase. It looks new and it's white and exactly what I had in mind. Wow, that intending stuff really works!" Kara is exactly right. The group magic of setting intentions that are good for you and also for everyone on the planet really does work. It took a month but I got everything on my list, too. Goddess is good. Friends are great.

Set Your Intention to Be a Master Manifestor

I learned the art of intention-setting some years ago and quickly incorporated it into my morning rituals. Upon waking, sometimes even before I open my eyes, I set my intention for the day—it only takes a minute! It can be about work, financial challenges, a problem I am dealing with, relationships, health, hopes and dreams—anything, as long as it is also for the good of all. It has become a morning prayer for me, quick and quiet. I simply state my intention, such as, "I intend that my presentation today at work will go really well and I will feel joy as it is happening and set the stage for success for this product launch, for the good of all. I am grateful for this wonderful day. And so it is." During the peak of my money woes, I would get very specific and set intentions for the exact amount of money I needed to make the mortgage payments, pay credit card bills, etc. Granular detail is good when manifesting so it is fine to say how much you want when intending with money.

Keep these other tips in mind:

* Avoid using words with any negative charge to them, such as "can't," "but," and "won't," and amplify your intention with a statement of gratitude immediately after.

* Always state your intention as if it is happening now and not in the future. Be specific and intend without limit.

* Your intentions do not always have to be personal to you and intending for the greater good of all contributes to a positive global shift.

* By setting intentions every day, you will soon become a master manifestor. I intend that for you!

Money-attraction Herbs

As a kitchen witch and gardening enthusiast, I am always seeking to learn more about how the power of herbs, plants, roots, and flowers can be used in the craft. Grow your wealth, literally, with these handy herbs.

* *Allspice berries* bring good luck: Gather seven berries and place in a small pouch to carry in your pocket or purse for a week. On the seventh day, place the berries in your fireproof dish and burn them with cinnamon incense while making your wish for whatever you want.

* *Basil* is a major herb of abundance as well as love. Drop a few fresh basil leaves on the floor of your kitchen and sweep them out of your home with your magical broom while speaking this charm: "Scarcity is out the door; no longer will I be poor. Health and wealth, be here now. Harm to none, so mote it be."

* *Cinnamon* has come to be called the "Sweet Money Spice" and this delightfully scented herb is a bringer of luck and will make a business more prosperous. Sprinkle a dash of ground cinnamon on the threshold of your front door, store, or business and watch the wealth walk in!

* *Cloves* are herbs of good fortune and even help in gambling. They also bring people together and bind them. If you need to turn your luck around, use cloves in spellwork as an herbal element or in incense or potpourri to create energy of abundance.

* *Ginger root* can speed up any magic. You can grind up the dried ginger root into powder; adding this to your money-attraction spells will bring the funds much sooner. Ginger tea brings money your way, briskly!

* *Nutmeg* is another spice beloved by gamesmen and gamblers. Carry a whole nutmeg in your pocket and your luck will improve the same day.

* *Thyme* is a common herb that will attract money to your home. Every time you cook with it you are drawing abundance and wealth toward you. Drink thyme tea for a quick fortune turnaround and fast money magic with this spell, "It is time for money to come my way; good luck is mine. Money thyme is mine with blessings for all."

Coin Conjuration

We all have unexpected expenses that come out of the blue—car repairs, medical bills, or helping a loved one in need. I had the latter with my family and had to reach deep into my coffers to heed the call. When you need to recover quickly financially, this coin spell will fill the bill, literally.

Gather together

- ☆ athame
- ☆ 3 gold (or yellow) candles
- ☆ frankincense or myrrh incense
- ☆ 3 yellow or gold-colored crystals, such as tiger's eye, amber, citrine, yellow jade, or another favorite of yours
- ☆ 3 pieces of yellow- or gold-colored fruit, such as yellow apples or oranges
- ☆ 13 coins of different denominations
- ☆ a green or gold jar with a lid

Timing: Perform this spell on the evening of a new moon or during a waxing moon phase.

Make a quickie temporary altar wherever you pay your bills and handle your money—maybe it is your desk or perhaps the kitchen table. Use your athame to create the circle of magic in this soon-to-be-sacred space. Place the candles, incense, crystals, and fruit on the temporary altar and arrange them into three groups so each group contains a crystal, piece of fruit, and candle. Light your candles and the incense. One by one, take the coins in your hand and pass them through the incense smoke. Place the coins in the jar. Now take the crystals in your hand and pass them through the smoke, then place in the jar and seal. Pick up one piece of fruit at a time and touch to your third eye (in the middle of your forehead). Pray aloud:

This offering I make as my blessing to all,
Comfort and earthly gifts upon us shall fall.
Fill my coffers with silver and gold.
In this time of great need, I will be bold.
For the good of all, young and old.
Fill my coffers with silver and gold.
And so it is.

Extinguish the candles and incense and place on your altar for future use, as well as the vessel containing the coins. When you go to sleep, dream of everyone you love, including yourself, receiving a harvest of material and spiritual wealth.

Magical Thinking: The Manifestor's Mindset

I first heard the wisdom of the visionary teacher and writer Louise Hay 25 years ago when my dear friend Duncan gifted me his well-worn cassette tape of her speaking about how to develop a mindset of abundance.

Duncan patiently explained to me his takeaways from Hay's wisdom. For example, when paying bills, instead of resenting the company that supplies your water and electricity, write the check, seal the envelope and say aloud, "Thank you [whomever your check is for], for supplying me with power for my home and trusting me to pay you. Blessings to you!" We began a ritual of walking together to the mailbox and pronouncing our gratitude to all the recipients of our money, adding the finishing touch of kissing the stamped envelopes and saying "Thank you!" before dropping them in.

Soon, it began to work for me, as I had a far better attitude about paying my bills. I realized that paying on time saved late fees and was finally able to budget and handle my money in a smarter way. Most surprising of all, I stopped being filled with dread and worry when bills came in and started paying them the same day they arrived, whenever possible.

That was in the early 1990s, when we walked to the mailbox for our 5-minute gratitude ritual. Nowadays with all the instantaneous ways of sending money and electronic payments, it might be closer to a 5-second ritual. However, you can still get into your manifestor's mindset and express thanks before you hit "send." The attitude of abundance that stems from this mindset is like a muscle; the more you use it, the stronger it will be and the more manifestation you will see.

Louise Hay is no longer with us but her brilliance and generosity of spirit remain and, thanks to all her books and audios, we can learn from her still.

Celebration of Plenty: *Morning Meditation*

True abundance comes from looking at what you have, rather than focusing on what you lack. This spell will begin each day with magic.

Upon waking, take time to reflect on the good things in your life. After meditating upon those blessings, say this spell aloud:

Today and every day,
I see the richness of life.
I thank you, Goddess,
For all the gifts and beauty in my world.
Today, I will share my blessings with others
and honor you.
I see plenty for all. Blessed be.

Luck by the Cup

When you are crafting money magic, it is good to get into the manifesting mindset with some prosperity tea.

Gather together

* ☆ 1 tablespoon dried rose hips
* ☆ 1 tablespoon dried chamomile
* ☆ 1 teaspoon orange peel
* ☆ 2 cups (480ml) freshly boiled water
* ☆ a teapot
* ☆ a green mug
* ☆ strainer
* ☆ 1 cinnamon stick

Steep the rose hips, chamomile, and orange peel in the freshly boiled water in the teapot for 4 minutes. Pour the tea into the mug through the strainer, and stir widdershins, or counterclockwise, with the cinnamon stick for a moment. As you drink, visualize the abundance coming into your life.

Finding Lost Treasure: *Potion of Plenty*

The humble dandelion, considered a bothersome weed by some, hides its might well. Dandelion root tea can help you find lost treasure, money, wallets, even people. When you drink it in direct moonlight, sleep will be sweet and clues and messages will appear in your dreams.

Gather together

* ★ mortar and pestle
* ★ 2 tablespoons dried dandelion root
* ★ 2 cups (480ml) freshly boiled water
* ★ a teapot
* ★ oven mitts
* ★ a large Pyrex bowl (or other heatproof bowl)
* ★ a strainer

With your mortar and pestle, grind the dandelion root and steep in the freshly boiled water in your teapot. Pour into the bowl through the strainer. Now slip on your oven mitts and hold the bowl in your hands. Say aloud seven times what you are looking for. Afterward, pour the potion onto your front stoop or the steps in front of your home. What you are looking for will return to you.

Money Magic Bath

You can almost seal the deal before a job interview with this prosperity ritual. This spell is most effective if practiced on a new or full moon Thursday night, but can certainly be used whenever you need.

Pour 6 drops of mint, verbena, or apple essential oil into running bath water. You can also use all three. Turn off all lights, step into the tub, and bathe by the light of a single green candle. As you close your eyes, meditate on your true desires. What does personal prosperity mean to you? What do you really need and what do you really want?

When you are clear about your answers, focus on the candle flame while whispering:

Here and now, my intention is set.
New luck will be mine and all needs will be met,
With harm to none and plenty for all.
Blessed be. So mote it be.

Cash in a Flash: Crystal Currency

Another charm for solvency is to take seven tiny turquoise stones in the palm of your hand and speak this wish-spell aloud:

Luck be quick,
luck be kind,
and, by lucky seven,
good luck will be mine.
Blessed be.

Place the seven small stones in your wallet or purse; more cash is on the way.

The Giving-tree Spell

In Celtic lore, certain kinds of trees were called wishing trees. Taoists refer to them as money trees; either way, they can be "giving" trees (see below).

Gather together

★ a plain white piece of paper

★ a pen

★ 1 stick of jasmine or rose incense

Write your wishes for prosperity and luck on the paper. Specificity is key and you should include the details of what you are asking for. If you need more money to buy a new laptop, write that down. It can be more than one wish. Now, fold your wish paper into a square as small as possible and bury the paper in soil at the bottom of a giving tree. Choose from the list of magical trees below, or trust your intuition in arboreal matters.

Light the incense stick, place it by the buried paper and pray aloud:

Tree of plenty; I ask you to give
More abundance and money so I can live,
I ask for _____ [fill in blank] as it will truly help me.
With harm to none, so mote it be.

Repeat the spell twice and your wish will be put into effect.

Giving Trees

* *Willow* for healing broken hearts

* *Apple* for divination and spellwork

* *Cherry* for romance

* *Oak* for strength and lust

* *Peach* for love magic

* *Olive* for peace

* *Aspen* for sensitivity

* *Eucalyptus* for purification

The Wealth of Wildflowers

Pagans revere poppies for their money magic. If you have a yard or any strip of ground you can garden, even a nearby meadow, buy poppy seeds and simply scatter half of them in early spring. Save the other half for the spell below. Soon, you will have a wealth of wildflowers. No doubt, you will be rewarded with the beauty and abundance of poppies for many years to come.

Gather together

* poppy seeds
* a small plain paper envelope
* a pen

Place the remaining poppy seeds in the envelope. Bless the envelope by chanting aloud:

Poppy, gold like the sun,
Thank you for the new fortune I've won.
With these words, this spell is sealed. And so it is.

Now, write the charm you have spoken on the envelope. Seal the envelope and place it in your wallet, behind your paper money. Your fortunes will begin to change as soon as the envelope is sealed.

Chapter 6

Express-lane Love Spells:

Attract, Create, and Keep Love in Your Life

My very first spellwork was on the subject of love at the request of a bestie. It might have worked almost too well when they eloped after a brief courtship, but it empowered me to believe I could wield the enchanted art. It seems fitting that my dabbling in love magic came from my own love for a dear friend. What better way to start down the enchanted path than with spells for love: spells that create the potential for love, draw the attention and devotion of a lover, strengthen the union between an existing couple, invoke sexual magic, heal a broken heart, and perhaps most importantly, fill your own heart with love and compassion for yourself? This chapter contains secret rites for aphrodisiacs, ritual celebrations for the high holidays of love, and insight into the mysterious realm of the moon and the stars. Why spend a Saturday evening alone when you already know the object of your desire? And why doubt your own power to attract love when a little herbal chemistry can make you virtually irresistible?

For maximum power, love spells require you to use herbs, crystals, the right colors and the correct timing with solar and lunar astrological signs, all with specific properties that correspond to your desired outcome. Luckily for you, we cover that well in Chapter 1 of this book.

First Moon of New Love: *Candle Bell Spell*

If you are in a phase of your life where you wish to attract new love,
try this Candle Bell Spell two days before the full moon.

Gather together

* ★ 1 pink votive candle
* ★ a tray
* ★ 1 long-stemmed red rose bud
* ★ a small hand bell
* ★ rose essential oil

Check your lunar almanac and on the first night of the full moon, place the candle on the tray on your altar. Lay the rose bud and bell beside the candle. Anoint the candle with the rose essential oil. For the next two nights, cup the candle in your hands and direct loving thoughts into its flame for at least 5 minutes. On the last night of the full moon, take a thorn from the rose and carve the name of your heart's desire into the candle wax, reciting:

I will find true love.
Light the candle and ring the bell thrice, saying:
As this candle begins to burn, a lover true will I earn.
As this flame burns ever higher, I will feel my lover's fire.

Ring the bell three more times and allow the candle to burn for a few minutes while gazing at the flame. Keep notes in your bedside journal or your Book of Shadows and note how long it takes for true love to walk into your life. It will be interesting to look back and see where it happens, what sign the moon and sun are in, and all the details that will inform your future magical workings.

Dreaming Devotion

This charm will help you see whether a newfound interest will become long term. If you lack clarity on this issue, your dreams can guide you. Use this talisman for clairvoyance.

Gather together

☆ a small red pouch

☆ 1 teaspoon each of dried lavender, dried thyme, and cloves

☆ bolline

☆ 1 vanilla bean pod

☆ 12 inches (30cm) red string or cord

Take the small red pouch and place the lavender, thyme, and cloves into it. Using your bolline, cut the vanilla bean pod into two pieces and place them in the bag. Now cut the red string or cord in two, using your sacred knife. Close the bag by tying it with the two sections of cord and hold the pouch in both hands until your warmth and energy fully infuse the potpourri inside. Recite:

Venus guide my dreams tonight—is he [or she] the one?
I dream of devotion and a lifetime of love.
Please give me your answers from the heavens above.
So mote it be. Blessed be.

Tuck your talisman under your pillow. Upon waking, think of your dream. You will receive your answer immediately.

Wanderful Invocation of Love

All of us want our home to be a welcoming place for love and contentment for ourselves and our significant other. You can greatly abet that outcome with this simple spell for binding love.

Gather together

* ★ 2 pink candles
* ★ rose essential oil
* ★ 2 long-stemmed pink roses
* ★ rose incense and incense burner
* ★ 2 rose quartz crystals, of any size
* ★ a tray to hold all these elements
* ★ your wand for love magic

Place all your ritual elements on the tray. Go to your bedroom and place the tray on your nightstand or another chest or table nearest your bed. Anoint your wand and both candles with the rose essential oil and place the roses and the quartz crystals beside the candles. Now light the candles and incense. Pick up your wand and intone aloud:

This is a place where joy lives.
This is a room where my heart gives.
Here is a temple to love and delight.
Here is a home filled with bliss and light.
Blessed be, and so it is.

With your wand, draw a heart shape twice in the wafting smoke of the incense while saying "I love _____." Stand, eyes closed, while visualizing you and your partner enjoying each other's company, happy and in love. End the ritual by saying: "Blessed be." I recommend keeping the tray in your bedroom where it can be a mini shrine to love.

Timing Is Everything: Love Signs

If you want to strike up a conversation with the handsome, shy fellow at work, try it when the sun is in *Gemini*, *Libra*, or *Aquarius*, the best times for communication.

If, after a few successful dates, you are looking for things to heat up, fix an aphrodisiac dinner one *Taurus* or *Scorpio* moon evening, the most sensual of times.

Declaring your true love will go very well during the fiery signs of *Aries*, *Leo*, or *Sagittarius*.

If you want to rekindle a long-lost love, try it when either the sun or the moon are in the signs of *Pisces* or *Cancer*, when sentiments run high. As ever, timing is everything, and certain days are made for love.

You'll have your best success in romancing an ambitious amour during the earthy signs of *Capricorn*, *Taurus*, and *Virgo*. You will probably find them while you are networking or building an empire.

Love Magic Wands

In the section "The Witch's Toolkit" you learned how to make your own wand (see page 12). Here is what you need to know about the perfect wand to use in rituals for romance:

* *Almond* is a sweet wood and smoother than many; it is excellent for love magic.

* *Beech* grants wishes, so be careful what you wish for!

* *Birch* is a wood that is very powerful for new beginnings.

* *Ivy wood* is related to women's mysteries and will bind people together.

* *Lilac* wands create beauty, harmony, happiness and bring you love.

* *Rosewood* makes the ultimate wand for spellwork conjuring true, lasting love.

Spell for New Beginnings

This spell can be used to meet someone new or to bring on a new phase
in an existing relationship.

Gather together

* ☆ 1 pink candle and 1 blue candle
* ☆ rose or jasmine essential oil
* ☆ 1 or more favorite flowers
* ☆ a bobby pin/hair grip or safety pin

Before dawn, anoint each candle with rose or jasmine essential oil and place them on your altar. Light both candles, lay the flower(s) next to them, and chant:

Healing starts with new beginnings, please show me who.
My heart is open, I'm ready now.
Today, my heart is open to love anew.
Goddess, you will show me how.
So mote it be.

Extinguish the candles and leave them on your altar. Pin the flower(s) to your lapel, jacket pocket, or in your hair and await the sweet message from the Goddess.

Spice Up Your Life Spell

Start a fresh chapter in your love life without delay with this cup of love.

Gather together

* ☆ cinnamon spice tea (from a shop) or 3 chopped cinnamon sticks
* ☆ 1 cup (240ml) of hot water
* ☆ 1 teaspoon honey
* ☆ 1 teaspoon ground cinnamon (or 3 more sticks ground in your mortar and pestle)

Brew and steep the tea for at least 3 minutes. Stir in the honey and savor the sweet, spicy smell. Drink it while contemplating your hopes, intentions, and dreams for a happy, healthy love life. Now, sprinkle the ground version of this charismatic spice on the threshold of your front door and along your entry path. When the cinnamon powder is crushed underfoot, its regenerative powers will help heat things up in your love life.

Spelling Love

Jasmine and rose have very powerful love vibrations to attract and charm a lover. This simple spell, said aloud, will create loving magic.

Gather together

* ★ 1 white candle
* ★ jasmine essential oil
* ★ rose essential oil

Anoint the candle with both essential oils and close your eyes. Say to yourself:

Venus, cast your light on me,
A goddess for today I'll be.
A lover, strong and brave and true,
I seek as a reflection of you.

Now open your eyes and gaze at the candlelight. Venus, goddess of love, has heard you.

Swipe Left for Love: *App Enchantment*

We all know many people find romance on dating websites and apps. Use your witchy tools of a pendulum (see page 11) and a whispered spell for swift and accurate swiping!

Still the pendant and hold it over the photo on the app of people who may be of interest to you, and then ask it to indicate yes and no. When you get a yes, swipe away! When you have found a person of interest, craft your first message to them, and speak this spell:

God of love, fly my letter hence at the speed of light.
May the arrow of love find a mate so right.
With harm to none and blessing for all.
And so it is.

Now, hit send. Make sure to have a charming response at the ready!

Attracting That Attractive Stranger:

Don't tell me you have never had a brief but meaningful encounter at your local café or exchanged long glances on the bus crossing town. Shyness tied your tongue, and now your only hope is that chance will bring you together. Try this trusty attraction spell.

Gather together

☆ a man-shaped mandrake root or substitute (see spell)

☆ 1 cup (20g) of red, white, and pink rose petals

☆ 1 red, 1 white, and 1 pink candle

☆ 2 goblets of red wine

Place the mandrake root (commonly available at herbalists and metaphysical shops) on your altar. If you cannot find the mandrake root, you could substitute any statue, drawing, photograph, or figure of a man that reflects some quality of your heart's desire. Surround the root or figure's base with the rose petals and candles. Place the goblets with a small amount of red wine in them beside the candles. Make sure it is a wine you really like and would want to share with a romantic interest, as you will refill the goblet each evening. Burn the candles for 5 minutes every night for a week, starting on Friday, Venus's Day.

Sip from one of the goblets, and recite:

Merry Stranger, friend of my heart,
Merry may we meet again.
Hail, fair fellow, friend well met,
I share this wine and toast you,
As we merry meet and merry part
And merry meet again.

Make sure you look your best when you step out as you will soon lock eyes again.

Oil of Love

Indulge in this sensually satisfying ritual concoction that will make your skin glow and will also surround you with a seductive aura. Your personal vibration will draw people toward you thanks to this lovely essence.

Gather together

* ⋆ 2 tablespoons (30ml) sweet almond carrier (or base) oil

* ⋆ 6 drops jasmine essential oil

* ⋆ 6 drops rose essential oil

* ⋆ 1 ounce (30g) aloe vera gel

* ⋆ 3-ounce (85ml) squeeze bottle

* ⋆ 1 tablespoon (15ml) rose water

* ⋆ 1 pink candle

* ⋆ 1 stick of rose incense

Timing: Perform this ritual on a moonlit night.

Place all the oils, rose water, and the aloe vera gel into your squeeze bottle. Shake the mixture well. As you undress, imagine you are preparing for the one you love. Light the pink candle and rose incense and say:

My heart is open, my spirit soars.
Goddess bring my love to me. Blessed be.

Now, pour the Oil of Love into your palm and gently rub into your skin. As you do so, dream of what delights are heading your way.

Ultimate Glamour

Few people know that the word "glamour" comes from the seventeenth-century Scottish word "glamour," which meant to cast a spell or enchantment over anyone who looks upon you.

During the waxing moon, take the rings, necklace, and earrings you are planning to wear during a special tryst and lay them on your altar to imbue them with magic. Mix together one tablespoon each of the dried herbs vervain, thistle, chamomile, and elderflower. Cover your jewelry with the herb mixture and then sprinkle salt on top. Leave for at least 5 minutes, then shake off the herbs and pick up your gems. Hold the jewelry in your hands and chant:

Bless these jewels and the hand and heart of the wearer with the light of heaven above.
May all who look upon me
See me through the eyes of love.

Now put on the empowered and enchanted jewelry and go off for your special date.

Enchanted Evening Rite

Take the time to prepare yourself for romance and turn your thoughts
to love and sensuality.

Gather together

* petals of 1 red rose
* a large glass or ceramic bowl and a wooden spoon
* ½ cup (90g) of Epsom salts
* ½ cup (70g) of baking soda
* ½ cup (120ml) carrier (or base) oil, ideally jojoba or apricot
* 6 drops each of jasmine, ylang ylang, and neroli essential oil (or 12 drops of one, if you prefer just one scent)

A soothing bath is the perfect prelude to your date. Make the water warm enough to be relaxing, but not so hot that it makes you sleepy. Mix all the ingredients, except for the rose petals, together in the bowl with the wooden spoon and then add the mixture under the running faucet. The Epsom salts will relax tense muscles and the baking soda combined with the carrier oil will soften your skin. These aphrodisiac essential oils are very potent. Lastly, float the rose petals in the water, and bathe by natural light before nightfall. As the mix of warm water, oils, and bath salts smooths your skin, let it also soothe your soul.

Passion Potion Massage Mix

Jasmine, neroli, amber, and just a touch of vanilla essential oils create
a romantic and exotic scent that lingers on your skin for hours.

Gather together

* ½ cup (120ml) unscented carrier (or base) oil, ideally jojoba
* ¼ cup (60ml) jasmine essential oil
* 10 drops amber essential oil
* 5 drops neroli essential oil
* 5 drops vanilla essential oil
* dark-colored, sealable bottle with a dropper cap

Mix all the oils together in the tightly capped bottle and keep in a dark cupboard. Passion Potion will last six months. Remember to always shake well before using.

Body Blissing Spell

If you want to share your Passion Potion with another, before you do, bless the mixture with this spell that will imbue any usage with an optimal loving experience:

Light of love, shine on us here
Help us to let go of any doubt and fear
Brighten all hearts with your light so clear.
Bring us all close, those we hold dear.
Light of love, love is near.
So mote it be.

Seal It with a Kiss: *Binding Love Potion*

When we are in love, we all hope for it to be requited. Spellcraft can help with that! Here's one to share with your lover.

Gather together

* ★ 2 teaspoons dried lemon balm, basil, blackberry, or magnolia buds
* ★ 2 cups (480ml) of water
* ★ a teapot
* ★ 2 mugs
* ★ honey, to sweeten

Quick Tip:
Beloved Besom: Symbol of Your Everlasting Love

If you and your spouse were joined in marriage with a traditional "old school" Wiccan handfasting, wherein you jumped over the broom, hang this besom in your bedroom near your bed. These besoms are often beribboned so use another ribbon as the hanger as you should not use a nail. This broom will serve as a happy reminder of your vows of love to each other.

To ensure a faithful relationship, make a tea from any of these herbs of loyalty in love. Boil the water and add to the teapot along with the herbs. Steep for 3 minutes, then pour the tea into the mugs and sweeten with honey. Intone this spell as you stir each cup.

Lover be faithful, lover be true.
This is all I am asking of you.
Give thy heart to nobody but me.
This is my will.
So mote it be.

Before you and your lover share this special treat together, whisper this wish in secret:

Honey magnolia [or whichever herb you chose], Goddess's herb,
Perform for me enchantment superb,
Let _____ [name of lover] and I be as one.
As ever, harm to none.

With this, the spell is done.

This spell must be sealed with a kiss between you and your beloved. Now enjoy drinking the tea with the object of your affection, from whom you wish not to stray, and his or her loyalty will never sway.

Brewing Up a Batch of Passion

For a passionate pick-me-up, drink this tasty tonic with your lover.

Gather together

- ☆ ½ cup (120ml) of lemonade
- ☆ 2 mugs
- ☆ 2 cups (480ml) of water
- ☆ ½ cup (50g) of sliced fresh ginger root
- ☆ 1 teaspoon cardamom
- ☆ honey, to sweeten

Pour half of the lemonade into each mug. Boil the ginger and cardamom in the water for 4 minutes, strain, then pour into the mugs and sweeten with honey to taste. Before you drink this lustful libation, simply say:

Gift of the Goddess and magic of moon,
May the flower of our love come to full bloom.

Shared between two lovers before a tryst, this enchanted potion will give great endurance for a memorable encounter. Each sip is full of love's sure power.

Spell for Letting Go

Most of us have had problems giving up on a relationship at one time or another.

Gather together

* ✦ a piece of black string, enough to tie around your waist
* ✦ bolline
* ✦ a photo or memento representing your ex

Timing: Ideally this should be done during the waning moon when things can be put to rest, but it works anytime you need it. Listen to your heart and you'll know exactly when it is required.

Tie the black string around your waist during the waning moon. Tie something symbolic from the old relationship to the end of the string —a photo or the name written on a scroll of paper, for example. Speak this spell aloud:

Bygones be and lovers part,
I'm asking you to leave my heart.
Go in peace, harm to none.
My new life is now begun.

Go outside and, using your sacred bolline, cut off the string and toss it away along with the memento where it will no longer inhabit your living space. You should feel freer and lighter immediately and will attract many new potential paramours now that you are not weighed down by lost love.

Cleansing Winds Heart-healing Rite

Helping a jilted friend get over a bad relationship is good medicine, which can be therapeutic for you, as well. Recently, a brilliant male co-worker of mine was "dumped" unceremoniously by a woman he had been seeing for two years. As I witnessed him sink quickly into a deep depression, I felt compelled to help by using this heart-healing rite. I knew my friend walked to work each day, so, following the spell, I scattered the petals of one flower near his office front door so he would step on them and release their curative powers. I left the other rose on his desk. His spirits improved that very day. The healing of his heart had begun and each day, he had more spring in his step.

Gather together

★ 2 long-stemmed white roses

Take the petals from one rose, and bless them, chanting:

Eastern wind, wild and free,
Help _____ [friend's name] to see,
A better love will come from thee.

Scatter the petals somewhere that your friend goes often, for example outside their house or place of work. Give the other rose to your friend.

New Moon Charm for Banishing Heartbreak

Any new moon is the perfect time to create a new opportunity. Clear away relationship "baggage" with this banishing spell. If you have been hurt emotionally, this will clear it, fast.

Gather together

* a clear glass bowl filled with 2 cups (480ml) of water
* a silver spoon
* a salt shaker
* palo santo incense
* 2 white candles and 2 black candles

Place the clear glass bowl of water on your altar. Set a silver spoon beside the glass bowl along with a salt shaker. Light the cleansing palo santo incense, the two white candles, and the two black candles. Pour salt on the spoon, sprinkle the salt into the water and stir with the spoon clockwise. Recite aloud:

Hurt and pain are banished this night;
Fill this heart and home with light.
With harm to none and blessings to all.
So mote it be.

After a few moments of contemplating the candle flames, recite the spell again. Using the silver spoon as a snuffer, extinguish the candles. Toss the bowl of water out on the street in front of your house, near a drainage grate. All your love troubles should drain away by the end of this lunar cycle.

Chapter 7

Rocking Your Life:

Crystals, Gems, and Supernatural Stones

Gems are powerful tools that can pave the way for a better life for you. There is a long history of the use of gems, stones, and crystals as amulets, symbols, charms, and jewelry in magic. These myriad stones can really enrich your life in so many ways. Do you want to get a new job? Jade jewelry magic will do the trick! Need to get over a heartbreak? A chrysocolla heart-healing spell will soothe your soul. Are you an author suffering from the dreaded writer's block? A creativity crystal incantation is exactly what you need.

Crystal magic also involves color magic and spellcraft, topics that are covered in depth herein. With crystal magic, you will learn to improve your life in ways large and small. You will discover the stones that are special to you and how to utilize fully birthstones and karmic crystals. You will undertake the magical arts of crystal conjuring and spell casting with stones. You will be inducted into the practice of healing with crystals and how to achieve wellness every day. Using gems and crystals in rituals, spells, and affirmations has been part of the human experience for millennia. By incorporating this practice into your life, you will create a flow of positive energy that will enable you to enhance your work, your family, your love, and every other part of your existence.

Yes, through the magic of gems, anything is possible. Again, welcome to this glittering and magical realm—I hope you're ready to begin a special journey under a sky where every star is a jewel you can wish upon!

Directing Your Destiny

By now, you may know exactly what kind of wood you want for your wand (see page 12). Now, you can select the ideal crystal to power your tool of magic. Below is a guide to the magical powers inherent in different crystals so you can choose which ones to use in your spells and rituals. Abundance rites will be enhanced with bloodstone or citrine while calcite and chalcedony offer protection. See which stones work best for you.

Supernatural Stones

* *Amethyst* for balance and intuition

* *Aventurine* for creative visualization

* *Bloodstone* for abundance

* *Calcite* for warding off ill fortune

* *Chalcedony* for power over dark spirits

* *Citrine* for motivation and success

* *Fluorite* for contacting fairies

* *Garnet* for protection from negativity

* *Hematite* for strength and courage

* *Jade* brings powerful dreams

* *Moss agate* for powers of persuasion

* *Quartz crystal* for divining your dreams

* *Rhodochrosite* for seeing life's true purpose

* *Watermelon tourmaline* for seeing the future

Lucky Wishing Charms

Many of us don't realize that the classic charm bracelet is decorated with magical symbols representing the wearer's wishes.

* For *prosperity*, such as before a job interview, when asking for a raise, or if you find yourself in arrears, wear a coin.

* For *love*, try a heart.

* For *creativity on a project*, a pen or artist's palette.

Silver Ring of Power Spell

A pure silver ring worn on the right pinky finger can bring both physical and psychic power. To enhance the magical power, have the ring engraved with your birth sign or astrological glyph and the sacred pentagram.

To instill the ring with protective power, clasp it over your heart and call out:

Ring of power, shield and encircle me. Blessed be.

Terrific Talismans: Personal Totems for Success

If you are preparing a major presentation to the team at work, showing your paintings to a curator, practicing for your dance performance, or pitching your book idea to a publisher, you can wear a talisman of your own making to ensure a positive outcome. Many performers, athletes, and musicians have lucky pieces of clothing or some token that gives them the courage to put themselves forth in the best possible manner. I have a Big Sur jade pendant on a length of leather that I wear on auspicious occasions such as these. Jade is about abundance and it is so smooth to the touch that it doubles as a soothing worry stone for me. I highly recommend you carry a jade talisman as it can be a major magical tool that can bring good fortune to you for many years.

To maximize the power of your jade talisman, consider the following tried-and-tested suggestions. Keep in mind that this will work even better if you place the item on your altar to imbue it with the right energy.

* For a speech, presentation, performance, or show, wear a *red* garment.

* If you are preparing for a potentially lucrative deal, you must wear *green*.

* If you are trying to empower someone to see and share your creative vision, *blue* is the right hue for you.

Walking the Pagan Path: *Stepping Stones*

For centuries, in group rituals and solo spells, witches have walked specific paths in the form of symbolic shapes that hold potent spiritual meaning. All you need for this ritual is a stone that brings you special inspiration.

Maybe it is your birthstone; perhaps it is your jade talisman or calming quartz or intuition-boosting amethyst or labradorite. Put the stone in your pocket and you are ready. You may find one walking pattern to be especially enriching for you. I recommend walking the figure eight, the "eternity" symbol from the magician card in the tarot deck. Otherwise, choose from among the universal shapes below. I suggest always walking sunwise, or clockwise. It can be a distance of your choice, in your living room, a bigger shape in your own backyard or whatever feels right to you, intuitively. For the more complicated patterns you can draw them on paper and place it where you can see it to use as a guide:

* *Oval:* The shape that designates the spirit and divine being.

* *Circle:* The shape of the sun and moon, designates the whole, the complete, that which never ends and encompasses all.

* *Cross:* The form of a human figure with arms outstretched from the center. The importance of this symbol predated Christianity by millennia.

* *Hexagram:* In the Jewish tradition, the beloved. It is two triangles intersecting, the meeting of heaven and earth.

* *Five-pointed Star:* This resembles the human form with arms and legs outspread—Leonardo Da Vinci's favorite.

Prepare for your pagan pilgrimage, your walking meditation, when the moon is in Sagittarius, Aquarius, or your natal moon sign. These prayer walks represent a journey to our own center and back again out into the world, some of the inner work we witches need to do now and again. (If you don't know your moon sign, consult an astrologer or one of the recommended resources on page 141.) Keep your eyes closed for the first step, then open your eyes and pray aloud:

Guide my steps; help me to walk in wisdom.
What I seek on this day, I shall find as I go
With an open heart and mind.
Today, I receive the blessings of the sun.

Quick Tip:
Ceremonial Crystal Knife

Athames, as you know, are not for cutting but for raising and managing energy. Athames that have been carved from crystals have become popular in recent years and can be very pretty. Consider these stones to be carved and polished and used as your sacred tool:

* *Amethyst* opens up psychic abilities.

* *Celestite* brings angel-powered insight and advice.

* *Selenite* is a stone of good fortune in the future.

* *Azurite with malachite* incites brilliance.

Crystal Feng Shui

Gems and statues positioned in strategic places around your home can help accelerate the positive vibrations you are activating by practicing crystal and gem magic.

Using what I call crystal feng shui, you can place a crystal or a geode or an appealingly shaped rock in the appropriate position in your home to facilitate change. For example, amethyst will promote healing and release any negative energy that is clinging. Clusters of citrine will activate vibrations of abundance and creativity.

So, if you want to bring more money into your home or office, place a big chunk of citrine on the left side of your desk, and the money will begin to flow! If you have a dark hallway that feels spooky or an area in your home or office where the energy feels very static or low, place an obsidian ball there, perhaps on a pedestal, to absorb this negative energy. If you want your bedroom to be a place of bliss and unconditional love, rose quartz will create this all-important atmosphere.

Crystalline Calm

You can create a sense of blissful and composed calm with the following spell.

Timing: The spell works best during early morning or twilight, when the light is half sun and half dark.

Sit with a turquoise stone for grounding in your left hand and with clear quartz in your right hand for calm and clarity. Feel the cool stones begin to warm to your hand and meditate in the quietude of half-light. Then speak this spell:

Fear and doubt leave me now.
Serenity and strength, come to me now.
In these stones, I feel the earth, the mountain.
I receive my vitality from Nature, grounding now.
Now and in the future, all joy will enter.
Harm to none, only good. Blessed be me.

Keep the two stones on your nightstand for whenever you need to regain calm and clarity.

Activate Your Third Eye: *Labradorescence*

Labradorite is a stunning stone with a lovely iridescence. As a magpie who is attracted to shiny objects, it grabs my attention every time. It can look as dull as dirt until you give it a closer examination; then you can see the glow under the surface. When cut and polished, it is fascinating and gorgeous, with an impressive light show of yellows, oranges, blues, and violets. In fact, the special play of light and color across the surface is called labradorescence. The effect is caused by lamellar intergrowths, produced inside the crystal while the crystal formed. Named after the place it was first found, Labrador, this loveliest of shiny objects can also be found in India, Finland, Russia, Newfoundland, and Madagascar.

As you might guess, this bluish feldspar is a soul stone with a very powerful light energy. It abets astral travel and connecting with the higher consciousness and is a favorite of mystics. It brings up nothing but positivity for the mind and excises the lower energies of anxiety, stress, and negative thoughts. It is an aura cleanser and balancer. Labradorite also protects against aura leakage wherein your personal energy drains out, leading to mental exhaustion and a case of the blues. This is a crystal to hold and keep with you during meditation, to enable psychic flashes, much like the flashes of light from within the stone.

I had no idea that it is also a stone that awakens psychic powers and activates your third eye until I learned this from the great teacher Scott Cunningham. Even a small piece of this special crystal will work. Take the crystal and hold it to the center of your forehead with both hands. Speak aloud:

Artemis, Astarte, Athena, Circe—fill me with your power,
On this day, I ask you lend me your seer's vision.
I stand at the threshold in this holy hour.
And so it is. Great goddesses; I am grateful.

Energy-clearing Spell

My friends probably start rolling their eyes when I enthuse about the latest crystal discovery, fossil find, or glamorous geode. I truly can't help myself as I simply love crystals and will never stop getting excited about these jewels that I consider to be major gifts from our Mother Goddess. She is endlessly generous and shows her love of us with the beauty and power of these sacred stones. Nevertheless, I do urge cleansing any and all new acquisitions so no unknown energy is allowed to permeate your home or impact your life or spellwork in any potentially negative way. All you need is a bowl of salt and you can cleanse your crystal and add it to your witch's toolkit.

Simply place the crystal in the salt, making sure every surface or facet is touched by the salt, and chant this charm:

Bones of our Mother,
Stone of this Earth,
Now your energy is clear.
Now your energy is clean.
Now your energy is here.
Blessed be.

Your new prize is now ready.

Soothsayer Stone: Choosing and Using a Crystal Ball

When selecting a crystal ball, your choice should not be taken lightly. This is a very personal tool that will become instilled with your energy. Crystal balls have their own authority and they can strongly influence the development of our psychic abilities.

You should think of the crystal as a container that houses your energy, so make sure it feels right for you. The crystal should feel comfortable to hold—not too heavy and not too light. You should not allow anyone else to touch your crystal ball. If someone does touch it, place the ball in a bowl of sea salt overnight to cleanse it of outside energy and influence. Quartz crystal balls have inherent power, so you have to practice working with them first. Pure quartz crystal balls can be quite expensive, but the price is worth it if you are serious about harnessing your intuition and using it for good. And don't expect your experiences to be like the movies! Most of the people I know who use crystal balls, including many healers and teachers, see cloudy and smoky images.

Work with a partner to sharpen your psychic skills. Sit directly across from your partner with the crystal ball between you. Close your eyes halfway and look at the ball and into the ball while harnessing your entire mind. Empty out all other thoughts and focus as hard as you can. You will sense your third eye, the traditional seat of psychic awareness, begin to open and project into the crystal ball. By practicing this way, you will train your mind. The patterns you see will become clearer and your impressions more definite. You should trust that what you are seeing is real and find a place of knowing. For me, my gut seems to be an additional center of intuition. I just "know in my gut" when something is amiss. Verbalize to your partner what you see, and then listen to your partner as they reveal their visions to you.

You should also do crystal ball meditations on your own. In a darkened room, sit and hold your crystal ball in the palms of both hands. Touch it to your heart and then gently touch it to the center of your forehead, where your third eye is located. Then hold the ball in front of your physical eyes and, sitting very still, gaze into it for at least 3 minutes. Envision pure white light in the ball and hold on to that image. Practice the white-light visualization for up to a half hour and then rest your mind, your eyes, and your crystal ball. If you do this every day, within a month you should start to become adept at crystal-ball gazing.

When we gaze into a crystal ball, it is possible to see into the fabric of time, both the past and the future. At first you may be able to see a flickering, wispy, suggestive image. Some of you may be able to see clearly defined visions on your first try. Most of us have to practice and hone our attunement to the energy of the ball. You must establish clearly your interpretation of what you see. Many psychics use a crystal ball in their readings, and some report seeing images of clients' auras in the ball. Projecting information about people's lives is a huge responsibility, so you need to feel sure about what you are reading. Learn to trust your body's center of intuition.

Darning Your Aura: *Crystal Combing*

We have all encountered psychic vampires, who tear away little pieces of your chi, or life force, leaving holes in your aura (etheric body). You can identify the places that need patching because they will become noticeably cold as you pass a crystal over them.

Pick your favorite stone from amethyst, citrine, or any quartz and run it all around you at a distance of about 3 inches (7.5cm). Make note of the cold spots and lay the crystal on those places for about 5 minutes, until the spot feels warmer. This repairs the holes in your aura and you should begin to feel a pleasant sense of renewed wholeness once again.

Another wonderfully soothing technique is crystal combing. Take a piece of pink kunzite and brush it in gentle, slow, downward strokes from the top of your head, the crown chakra, to the bottom of your feet. The next time you feel overwhelmed by anxiety, try this and you will feel more relaxed and in control afterward.

Kunzite is also a heart mender, which works with the heart chakra to bring inner peace, clear away old romantic wounds, and get rid of emotional baggage. While lying down you can place a chunk of kunzite upon your chest, meditate with it, and feel the healing energy flow in.

Prompt Prophecies: *Crystal Divination*

Give your tarot cards a rest and create a one-of-a-kind divination tool: a bag of crystals you can use to do readings. It is very easy to do. Collect together the stones you have picked up on your travels, and keep your eye out for crystals as you go about your daily business. You can also acquire relatively inexpensive stones, such as garnets, agates, amethysts, and tiny citrines, at your favorite metaphysical shop or you can buy them online (see Resources, page 141). Ideally you would have all the stones listed opposite, but if you don't, you should have at least a dozen to start with.

I have used this divination tool for matters ranging from career, wealth, health, love, and travel. Once I asked about staying at a job where I was increasingly unhappy and pulled out tiger's eye, amethyst, and quartz. The crystals were telling me that dishonesty was involved on some level and a shift would soon be revealed. That was all I needed to initiate a new job hunt as quickly as possible. Happily, and with the help of prosperity magic in this book, I landed a more lucrative new position. Shortly after I left, a former colleague contacted me to say that bankruptcy was in the works because of years of financial chicanery. Listen to the messages of crystals!

Select a favorite velvet bag, and when the need arises, turn to crystal visions for your enlightenment. Most of us cannot afford diamonds in our bag of crystals, so substitute with clear quartz here; for emeralds, switch to peridots, and garnets can substitute nicely for rubies. Some New Age stores and online sources also have "rough rubies" and "rough emerald" pieces for just a few dollars each, so it is possible to find these spiritual stones at reasonable prices.

Casting the stones is as easy as one, two, three:

1. Shake the bag well.

2. Ask a question.

3. Remove the first three stones you touch, and then interpret them with the following guide.

Crystal Meanings

* *Amethyst:* change is coming

* *Black agate:* monetary gain

* *Red agate:* long life and health

* *Aventurine:* new horizons and positive growth

* *Blue lace agate:* the need for spiritual and physical healing

* *Citrine:* the universe offers enlightenment

* *Diamond:* stability

* *Emerald:* lushness

* *Hematite:* new prospects

* *Jade:* everlasting life

* *Red jasper:* the need for grounding

* *Lapis lazuli:* heavenly fortune

* *Quartz:* clarity where there was none

* *Rose quartz:* love is in your life

* *Ruby:* deep passion and personal power

* *Sapphire:* truth

* *Snowflake obsidian:* your troubles are at an end

* *Tiger's eye:* the situation is not as it appears

* *Snow quartz:* major changes

Monday	Tuesday	Wednesday	Thursday	Friday	Saturday	Sunday

Chapter 8

Time Is On Your Side:
Making the Most of Every Sacred Day

Whether we are conscious of it or not, our lives are centered around ritual. The Wednesday night pizza and a movie with the kids is a family ritual. The Saturday night date is a romantic ritual; going to your favorite yoga for a spiritual and physical workout is a self-care ritual; and the growing trend Sunday knitting circles are a wonderful community ritual. We need ritual to inform and enrich our lives, to deal with stress, and above all, to create meaning in our lives.

In this chapter, my aim is to encourage you to incorporate magic into your life anytime you wish. We Wiccans often perform rites on high holidays or on new moons or celestial events, but your life will be all the richer if you do spellwork and rites "when the spirit moves you." Perhaps you are feeling as if you are in a bit of a rut and need change. Or, you might be having problems at work, or want to take your career to the next level. Spellcraft can help— start this week! You can do life-changing magic all year round with the tips, tools, and spells in this book. Take the best to heart, those that really resonate with you, and apply them to your life. Ritual is very much a part of our history and should be studied and applied to our lives today. It gets us out of our heads and back into our bodies; it gets us into a place of spirit. By participating in rituals on a regular basis, you can grow in wisdom and feel an increasing sense of your aliveness. The following rites and rituals can be done anytime, but their power is enhanced when practiced on the suggested days.

Mondays Are Made for Magic

Monday comes from "moon day" and is ruled by the moon goddess known variously as Diana, Cybele, Artemis, and Selene. This first day of the work week is associated with all the hues of blue, from sapphire to pearly iridescent. This is the day for intuition, deep reflection, and love, especially loving your own true nature.

Your Psychic Shield

You would not leave your house on a cold windy day without a sweater or jacket, right? I highly recommend you do not leave your house on a Monday morning without a psychic shield—you'll thank yourself later. If every work week feels like a challenge with a huge workload, tons of meetings, presentations, calls, and interactions, you should erect a protective shield so you can do good work but emerge unscathed from all busyness and business with others.

Visualize whatever feels like a secret defense against unwarranted psychic intruders. Some folk see big castle doors or a drawbridge, others utilize an enclosing egg, and I have even heard of a big silver blanket as a shield, but I prefer a kind of "force field" shield that I put up or take down. I also use a mental hooded robe that I wear anytime I go out in a group where I feel unsure about the people. In my mind, I cloak myself in my silver robe and do a brief silent meditation. Also, the best defense is a strong, positive attitude and sense of self. The more you practice your meditation and creative visualization, the greater your skill will grow.

The Sacred Seven

This simple spell acknowledges the life force and the cycles of nature that give rise to our creativity.

On a Monday, light seven purple candles to represent the days of the week, and say aloud:

We begin by honoring the sun;
We begin by honoring the light.
We light these candles for our friends,
Our families, those we love.
May the light of these candles draw the power
of nature into our hearts;
May the light of the candles inspire us to help and never harm;
May each of the seven days be radiant with the
Light from every start.
Blessed be.

Extinguish the candles and keep them for another Monday ceremony.

Tuesdays Are for Magical Plans

Named after the Norse god, Tiw, Tiw's day is ruled by Mars, the god of war and action. This day wears the colors red and pink. Like the old saying, "Tuesday is good news day," this day is auspicious for matters regarding prosperity, truth, new beginnings, and high energy with focus.

Good Impression Incantation

Are you going for an interview, attending an important meeting, or speaking to your new editor? Clearly, you will want to make the best impression when launching this important new relationship. To ensure that you start on the right footing, let the enchantment begin!

Gather together

* ☆ 1 orange candle
* ☆ 1 yellow apple
* ☆ 5 pumpkin seeds
* ☆ a citrine or clear quartz

All of these objects contain the properties of sharpness, intelligence, and clarity.

In the first light of a Tuesday morning, place the items on your altar. Light the orange candle and eat at least half of the apple and all the pumpkin seeds. Ancient Romans called our sun Sol and viewed it as an invincible life-bringing force. Meditate and visualize the beginning of your successful encounter and watch as the glow of sunshine fills the room with the radiant energy of the yellow-orange sun. Chant:

Sol, I bask in your bountiful rays,
this and all days.
As you shine, so shall I.
So mote it be.

Snuff out your candle and be prepared for a productive new relationship that will carry your work to new heights.

The Sacred Flame

Here is a marvelous way to "reset" and forge a new path for yourself with fire, best done on a Tuesday.

Gather together

* your cauldron or an outdoor firepit or grill

* sage for smudging

* athame

* several pieces of paper and a pen

Light a fire in your fire-safe vessel, then light the sage and smudge the area well. With your athame, draw the magic circle around your fire circle. Sit around the fire, relax, and think about what challenges you face and need to overcome in your life.

Write on a separate piece of paper each issue that comes up for you. Then, with great intention, place each piece of paper on the fire. Take a moment of silent meditation, and on a new piece of paper write your hopes for the future. Fold this paper and carry it with you in your purse or wallet. Your vision for the future will take on a life of its own. End the ritual with another sage smudging and make sure the fire is completely out before you go back inside.

You should perform this rite at least once a year.

Wednesday Is We Day

The very word Wednesday comes from the old German name for the supreme god, Woden. Woden's day is associated with the winged god of communication, Mercury, whose colors are yellow and green. This is an optimal time to try something new or make a new contact. Wednesday stands for strength, joy, theatrics, extravagance, and great staying power.

Communing with Your Coven

The path of Wicca can often feel solitary, but it doesn't have to be. Witchcraft, which is in itself highly creative, is even more so when practiced in a supportive circle. Wednesdays are wonderful for getting together with like-minded folks. Invite four of your fellow pagans over.

Gather together

* ☆ a censer or incense burner
* ☆ 2 green candles
* ☆ 2 yellow candles
* ☆ palo santo incense

Place the ritual elements on a table that will serve as an altar. Stand in a circle near the altar, holding a censer or incense burner. Ask each of your guests to represent one of the four directions: north, east, south, and west. Give the people representing north and south green candles and east and west get yellow. Light the incense and bless each candle with the sweet-smelling smoke.

Bless the candle of the East, saying:
Inspired by air.

Bless the candle of the West saying:
Burnished by fire.

Bless the candle of the North, saying:
Cleansed by water.

Bless the candle of the South, saying:
Strengthened by earth.

Together, everyone chants:
Blessed be.

After the ritual, sit in a circle and share your ideas and creative vision. Talk about how you can support each other in realizing your full potential.

The Secrets of Seers: *Prophecy Potion*

If you and your circle, coven, or group want to increase your abilities to intuit and invent together, brew up a batch of creative juices at a Wednesday gathering.

Gather together

* ½ cup (30g) of dried herbs: kava kava, borage, mugwort, yarrow, or dandelion

* 4 cups (960ml) of freshly boiled water

* a large teapot

* 4 mugs

Steep the herbs in the freshly boiled water in your teapot for 4 minutes, then pour the tea into the four mugs. Before your group begins drinking, say:

Goddess of the Oracles, please give us the sight!
God of the Prophets, please give us the vision!
Fate of the Future, we call on you for truth.
Harm to none, so mote it be.

Notice we did not mention to strain the herbs. In addition to the dreams, visions, and all you will soon foretell, you can begin with these cups of aromatic herbs and read the tea leaves by interpreting the shapes you see at the bottom of the mug once you have drunk the liquid.

* *An apple* symbolizes knowledge or success in studies.

* *A candle* indicates wisdom and enlightenment.

* *A cat* can mean you have a deceitful friend.

* *A dog* can mean you have someone loyal in your life.

* *Flying birds* represent a letter bearing a happy message.

* *Ravens* are an omen of troubles ahead.

* *A shamrock* shows a wish will come true.

* *Kite shapes* show good news flying to you.

* *A letter of the alphabet* references a person whose name starts with that letter.

Thursdays Will Bring You Good Fortune

Thursday is an excellent day for manifesting. Thursday is named after Thor, the recently popular Norse god. Turn to Thor when you need to use spirituality as an approach to solve a legal matter. He is also a powerful protection deity to invoke in ritual. You can and should do prosperity rituals every Thursday through prayer and offerings to this ancient god of abundance. He is the equivalent of the Greco-Roman god Jupiter, or Jove. These generous deities can always be counted on to deliver.

Visualizing Your Bright Future: *Jovial Enchantment*

As the sun sets on a Thursday, you can connect to the god of all good things who can shine his bright light on your accomplishment and productivity. Thursdays are ruled by Jupiter and the color of this day is blue.

Gather together

* mortar and pestle
* ½ teaspoon each of amber resin and patchouli
* a censer or fireproof clay or glass dish
* 1 blue candle
* amber essential oil

With your mortar and pestle grind together the amber resin and patchouli. Burn this incense in your censer or on a piece of charcoal in a fireproof dish. Anoint a blue candle (for expansion and Jovial energy) with amber essential oil. Light the candle and meditate on the flame, inhaling deeply the scent of the warm and sweetly fragrant amber oil. As you meditate, think about how you sometimes doubt yourself and your instincts. Visualize clearing that from your mind. Think about your talents and your potential as you chant:

Jupiter, great god in the sky
as you may flourish, so do I.
Right now, under your blue light,
I see my future and it is bright.
And so it is.

Blow out the candle and cast both it and the incense ash remnants into a fireplace or your cauldron. You must completely destroy the candle, as it contains the energy of your inner critic.

Support from Afar

We all have friends and loved ones who live many miles away but who need our support. Long-distance magic can be quite effective so, on a Thursday, try this ritual with your group. It has worked really well for my spiritual circle.

Gather together

★ a photo of the friend in need or other symbol to represent that person

★ a small hand bell or chime

★ a vase of yellow flowers

★ a piece of paper and a pen

Take the photo of your friend or the symbol that represents him or her, for example a gift he or she has given, or even a business card, and place it on a pedestal or table. Surround it with a small hand bell or chime and a vase filled with one or more of these "flowers of fortune:" nasturtiums, golden poppies, daisies, yellow roses, or your friend's favorite happy posy.

Take a piece of parchment and write your friend's full name. Speak the following spell:

On this earth and under these stars, I call upon the gods and goddesses to bring great help and good fortune to _____ [your friend's name].

Ring the bell or chime.

In this air and through these waters, speed here in the name of _____.

Ring the bell or chime again.

Through the fire and through the rain, bring aid, goodwill, and bright blessings to _____ now.

Ring the bell or chime again.

As a group, send the positive energy to your friend across the miles by saying, "We love you, ____", and ring the bell vigorously one last time.

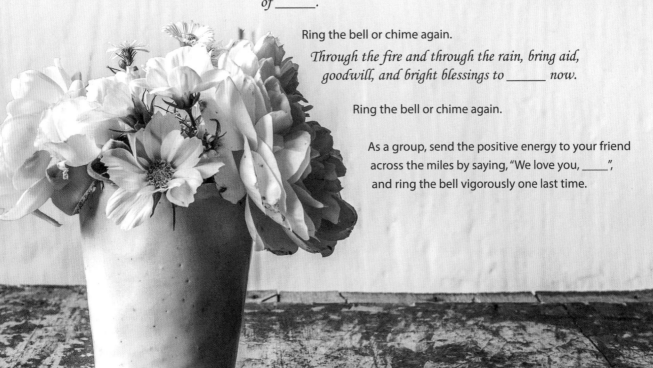

Fridays Are Festivals

Friday might be the favorite night of the week, as well it should be, since Friday is associated with Venus, the goddess of love, and Freya, the powerful goddess also associated with love in the Norse pantheon. As such, Fridays are the time to get out and be social, whether it be date night, girls' night out, or a lovely dinner with family and friends. Be with people and express yourself, laugh, and be merry.

Magic Amplified: *Prayer for Pagan Partnership*

Perhaps what you need most is a partner to support, encourage, and collaborate with in your magical workings. On a waxing moon Friday night, this spell will bring your partner to you.

Gather together

* ☆ 1 lemon
* ☆ 1 orange
* ☆ 2 rosemary sprigs
* ☆ 1 orange candle
* ☆ a fireproof clay or glass dish

Group the fruit and rosemary around the orange candle. Light the candle and intone:

On this night
I do invite
new energy to bring delight
Under this lunar light. So mote it be.

Now, using the candle flame, light the tip of the rosemary sprigs and set them in the fireproof dish. Rosemary has a very powerful cleansing smoke. It was used as an incense by ancient priests and priestesses in Greek and Roman times and by prophets and seers. It cleanses the aura and paves the way for major magic. Soon your partner in spellwork will appear.

Moon Sister Smoke

To strengthen the bond between you and your gal pals, share
this rite of friendship and fun on a Friday night.

Gather together

☆ a bottle of red wine

☆ goblets for all

☆ pink and purple candles,
   1 for each person

☆ rose and vanilla incense,
   1 stick per person

☆ a large tray to hold everything

☆ incense burners

Sit on the couch around a table or in a circle on the floor among cozy pillows. Place the wine bottle, goblets, candles, and incense on the tray in the center of your group. Each participant lights a candle and a stick of incense. Wave the incense around and put in a burner on the tray. Now pour the wine into the goblets and pray aloud so your guests can hear you:

Daughters under the sun,
Sisters under the moon,
Tonight we bind our hearts and minds.
So mote it be.

Speak the spell twice, hand each participant a goblet of wine and then toast each other. Let the merriment begin! You can change the wording of this spell for gender.

Saturdays Are for Me-time

Associated with black, white, and gray, Saturday is the day of the ruling judge Saturn. This is when we must take stock of the week, get errands and personal business done, and finish the day off with a decorous meal with friends and loved ones.

Sacred Self-care: *Relaxation Massage Oil Blend*

Weekends are the best time for taking good care of yourself. We all need to practice self-care more than ever now that the world seems so chaotic and life is crazy-busy. Sandalwood, lavender, and clary sage create a deeply soothing blend with a sensuous scent. It is both restful and stimulating—the perfect combination.

Gather together

* ☆ 6 drops sandalwood essential oil
* ☆ 6 drops lavender essential oil
* ☆ 6 drops clary sage essential oil
* ☆ ½ cup (120ml) jojoba or almond carrier (or base) oil
* ☆ dark-colored, sealable bottle with a dropper cap
* ☆ 1 cup (240ml) warm water

Put the essential oils and carrier oil into the dark-colored, sealable bottle. Carefully cap the bottle and gently shake until the oils have blended together. Store the bottle in a dark cupboard. Before using it on yourself or a loved one, shake well. You can warm it by putting the sealed bottle in a cup of warm water and let it sit there for 4 minutes. Many masseuses pour the oil into their palm and let their own body heat warm it. Either way adds to the relaxation factor.

Saturday Spell for Contacting Spirits

Outside of the witchy world, it is not well known that Saturday is the optimal day for contacting those who have passed from this realm to the next. When Samhain, to mark the end of the harvest season, falls on a Saturday, it gives a big boost to our ability to make contact through the veil between the worlds. After nightfall, you can speak to lost loved ones or others with whom you desire contact.

Gather together

* an amethyst of the deepest, darkest purple, obsidian, and/or rainbow moonstone (see spell)
* your Book of Shadows and a pen
* strong-smelling incense, such as frankincense, nag champa, or sandalwood
* a fireproof clay or glass dish
* sage for smudging

You can either use one of each of the three crystals, or three of the same kind of crystal. Sit in a comfortable position on the floor or on a pillow with your Book of Shadows and pen nearby. I learned from High Priestess Z. Budapest that "the dead love incense, the stronger the better and it will call them to you." Light the incense in the fireproof dish and pass the crystals through the smoke. Then touch your third eye with one of the crystals for a moment and picture the person you want to contact. Place that crystal by the dish of sweet-smelling smoky incense. Take the other two crystals in your hand and speak this spell aloud:

Great Goddess, I call _____ [speak the name of the spirit] forth now.
From this side, to you, will I bow.
Words of wisdom, we need here and now.
Peace and love is here, I vow.
With harm to none, Blessed be thou.

Now pass your Book of Shadows through the incense smoke and start writing down the messages. Whatever comes into your mind is what you are meant to know. After a few moments, thank the spirit and say goodbye, directing it back to its side of the veil. Extinguish the incense and light the sage and give a very good smudging to the area. Place your Book of Shadows on your altar and consider the message this generous spirit has given you.

Sundays are for Basking in the Warmth

Sunday is the day of our greatest star, Sol, otherwise known as the sun, with colors of gold, orange, and radiant white. This is the time to rest and renew, indulge in creativity, and enjoy the fruits of this life. Sunday is the time to make spells for fame and fortune.

Magical Affirmations

Sundays are an ideal time for boosting your confidence and esteeming yourself.

On a Sunday morning after your ablutions, when you are your most well-rested, freshly scrubbed, shiniest self, speak these powerful words:

I am amazing and awesome
I grow in wisdom each day.
I am succeeding.
I am prospering.
Blessings to all and blessed be me.

Feel free to create your own affirmations, if you are so inspired. This Sunday ritual feels simply divine and truly is empowering. If it works as well for you as I suspect it will, you may want to incorporate it into every Sunday morning. Blessed be!

Sanctified Sunday: *Sure Success Incantation*

Here is one of the ways I got a great job on my first day in San Francisco, despite the fact that I wasn't really qualified and looked like an absolute hayseed after driving cross-country for four straight days from Appalachia. I was broke and fresh out of grad school with no real experience but I created some luck for myself. You can, too, with this surefire spell.

Light a gold candle on a Sunday night before you undertake your job hunt or whenever you are about to go on a job interview. Repeat this incantation three times while holding a vision of your desired job:

I see the perfect job for me; I see a place of plenty.

Upon my heart's desire, I am set;

My new boss will never regret.

This job will come to me NOW.

Harm to none I VOW.

So mote it be.

Conclusion:
Fill Your Life with Enchantment

We are experiencing a witchy renaissance here in the early years of the twenty-first century. I get frequent requests from friends and, thanks to the quick connections of social media, questions via Facebook about how to handle the stress, strain, and busyness of modern life. I am honored to be able to help in any small way and am constantly seeking new methods for healing magic and insights and spells for sacred self-care.

One thing I do know, both from my personal experience and from my circle, is that spellwork and habitual ritual can be healing in and of itself. Rites and ritual gatherings regulate our lives, individually and as groups. Anthropologists, psychologists, and other students of the human race have shown that ritual has existed since the dawn of humanity and has always played an important role in culture. Scholars of the psyche, including Freud, who eloquently addressed the role of ritual, speak of the power of ritual and how it brings people together physically and emotionally. Ritual creates "communities" from which spring a sense of unity, harmony, and belonging.

These magical moments are very important; they signify that we have stepped out of the routine of the ordinary day to day and are exploring a higher consciousness. I believe a moment spent in ritual is embracing life itself. Even 5 minutes of sacred time can change your life for the better. And that is my hope for you: a life enriched through these easy enchantments and simple spells. May you enjoy much peace of mind, prosperity, love, and sheer joy!

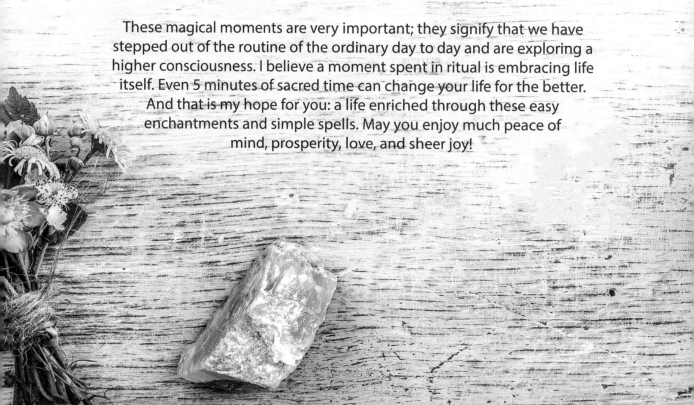

Resources

Moon Phases and Lunar Astrology

Moon phases, Sun and Moon signs, and more: almanac.com/topics/astronomy/moon/moon-phase

The Old Farmer's Almanac is also available in print: store.almanac.com

Lunar lore, herbal lore, and astrological information: thewitchesalmanac.com

I also recommend *Llewellyn's Daily Planetary Guide* (published annually for the year ahead).

Crystals

Crystals, Tibetan rock salt, fossils, gems, and jewelry: crystalsbynature.com

Crystals, wands, crystalline statuary, and jewelry: crystalage.com

Petrified wood and fossils: www.fossilera.com/fossils-for-sale/petrified-wood

Birthstones, crystals, and lore: birthstonemagic.com

Essential Oils, Incense, and Herbs

Advice on using essential oils safely: www.aromaweb.com/articles/safety.asp

Essential oils, carrier oils, and soap- and candle-making supplies: junipertreesupplies.com

Incenses, burners, sages, and herbs: herbsandarts.com/incense-burners

Dried herbs, essential oils, floral waters, and books: scarletsage.com

Four Major Sabbats:

Candlemas—February 2
Beltane—May 1
Lammas—August 1
Samhain—October 31

Four Lesser Sabbats:

Vernal Equinox—March 20
Summer Solstice—June 24
Autumn Equinox—September 23
Winter Solstice/Yule—December 21

A Witch's Calendar: Additional Sacred Days Celebrating Women

January 6—Feast of Goddess Sirona, the blessing of the waters

January 11—Carmentalia, a woman's festival celebrating women's mysteries, prophecy, and birth

February 2—St Brigid's Day when new witches are initiated with the waxing of winter light

February 14—Aphrodite's Week, a festival of love (now Valentine's Day)

March 30—Feast of Fertility, a rite of spring for planting and sowing

April 28—Festival of Flora, rituals of abundance for new flowers and vegetables

June 1—Festival of Epipi, an exhortation of the Full Moon and her mysteries

June 7—Vestalia, the festival of Vesta, the Roman goddess of home and hearth

July 7—Nonae Carpotinae, ancient Roman custom celebrating women, feasting under the fig tree

August 13—Festival for Diana, huntress and moon goddess, worshipped with fires and pilgrimages

August 21—Consualia, greeting the coming harvest with dances, feasting, song, and sport

December 19—Opalia observes Ops, the ancient goddess of farmers and fertility

Index

Acknowledgments

Deep gratitude to publisher Cindy Richards and CICO Books for the great pleasure of working on this book, which is a thing of beauty and a visual delight. Belle Daughtry's photography and styling are brilliant and offer so much to readers. Big thanks to Eliana Holder for her elegant design. The layout is simply wonderful. I greatly appreciate how copy-editor Sophie Elletson spun my words into gold.

The true magicians here are duo Carmel Edmonds and Kristine Pidkameny. Without them, none of this could happen and I am one lucky writer to have the honor of working with these two wise and wonderful women. CICO Books publishes works of art and I am grateful to all of them for the care and craftsmanship they put into their publications.

Photography credits

All photography is by Belle Daughtry apart from the following:

p. 38: Clare Winfield
pp. 42, 118, and 137: Crystal photography by Roy Palmer
pp. 54, 136, and 138: Kate Whitaker
p. 134: William Reavell